THE 100+ SERIES™

Reproducible Activities

Math

Grades 3–4

Published by Instructional Fair
an imprint of
Frank Schaffer Publications®

Instructional Fair

Editors: Melissa Warner Hale, Melissa Hale

Frank Schaffer Publications®

Instructional Fair is an imprint of Frank Schaffer Publications.

Send all inquiries to:
Frank Schaffer Publications
8720 Orion Place
Columbus, Ohio 43240-2111

Math—grades 3-4

ISBN 0-7424-1721-2

6 7 8 9 10 11 MAZ 09 08 07 06

Table of Contents

Number and Operations
Place Value 4–6
Rounding. 7
Addition 8–14
Addition Problem Solving 15
Subtraction. 16–22
Subtraction Problem Solving 23
Multiplication. 24–31
Multiplication Problem Solving . . . 32
Division 33–40
Division Problem Solving 41
Mixed Operations 42–43
Averaging 44–45
Fractions 46–50
Decimals 51–52
Money. 53–54

Pre-Algebra
Shape Patterns. 55
Number Patterns. 56–57
Missing Values. 58–59
Number Letters. 60
Number Pyramids 61
Find the Rule 62
Pre-Algebra Problem Solving 63

Geometry
What's a Polygon?. 64
Types of Triangles 65
Quadrilaterals 66
Types of Polygons. 67
Identifying Polygons 68
Dimensions 69
Pyramids and Prisms. 70
Cones, Cylinders, and Spheres . . 71
Classifying Prisms. 72
Congruent or Similar?. 73
Symmetry 74
Reflection and Rotation 75
Lines, Line Segments, and Rays . . 76
Parts of a Circle 77
Coordinate Graphing 78
Using a Grid 79–80

Measurement
Types of Angles 81
Time Angles. 82
Time Word Problems 83
Time Conversions 84
Perimeter 85
Area 86
Area and Perimeter 87
Area of Triangles, Rectangles, and
    Parallelograms 88
Estimating Area 89
What Is Volume? 90
Find the Volume. 91
Using a Rule to Find Volume . . . 92
Temperature 93–94
Measure Me 95
Customary Units of Length 96
Metric Units of Length. 97
Selecting Appropriate
    Units (Metric) 98
Customary Units of Capacity. . . . 99
Metric Units of Capacity 100
Selecting Appropriate Units
    (Capacity) 101
Customary Units of Mass 102
Metric Units of Mass 103
Selecting Appropriate Units
    (Mass) 104

Data and Probability
Pictograph 105
Tally Chart. 106
Venn Diagram 107
Glyph 108
Circle Graph 109
Line Graph 110
Representing Data Different Ways 111
Median, Mode, and Range 112
Probable Outcomes 113–114
Relative Frequency 115
Degree of Likelihood 116–117

Answer Key 118–128

Place Value

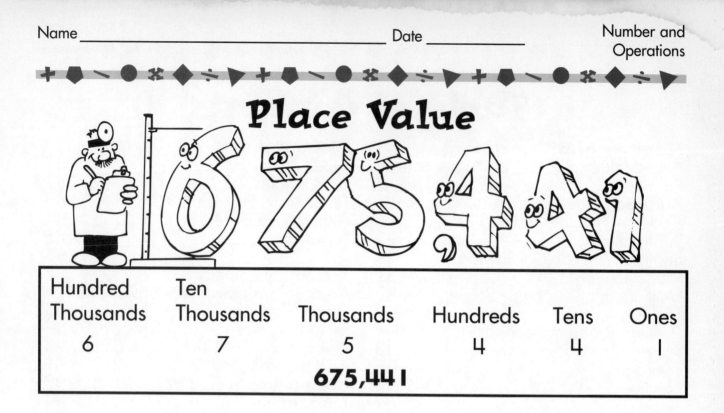

Hundred Thousands	Ten Thousands	Thousands	Hundreds	Tens	Ones
6	7	5	4	4	1

675,441

▶ Draw a line to match the numbers with the words.

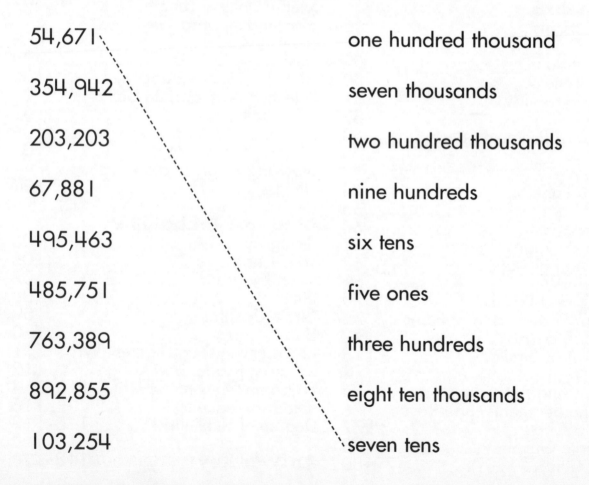

54,671   one hundred thousand

354,942   seven thousands

203,203   two hundred thousands

67,881   nine hundreds

495,463   six tens

485,751   five ones

763,389   three hundreds

892,855   eight ten thousands

103,254   seven tens

Place Value

▶ Use the clues to write a number in each box.

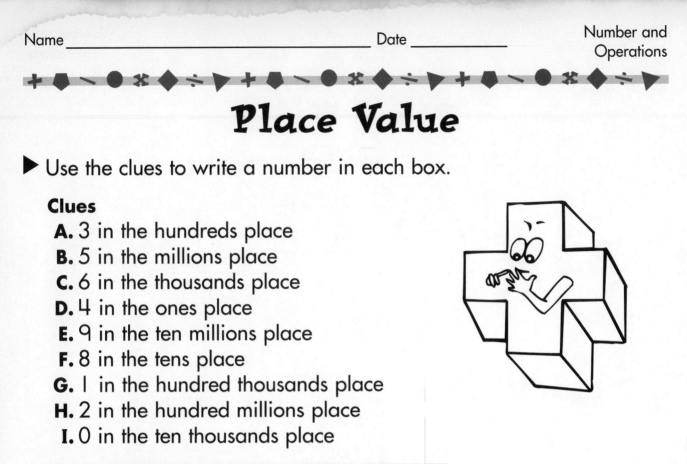

Clues

A. 3 in the hundreds place
B. 5 in the millions place
C. 6 in the thousands place
D. 4 in the ones place
E. 9 in the ten millions place
F. 8 in the tens place
G. 1 in the hundred thousands place
H. 2 in the hundred millions place
I. 0 in the ten thousands place

Millions			**Thousands**					

▶ Write numbers to make the sentences true.

1. In 2,648, the number _____ is in the tens place.

2. In 6,397, the number _____ is in the hundreds place.

3. In 6,873,251, the number _____ is in the hundred thousands

place.

4. In 3,789,251, the number _____ is in the thousands place.

5. In 8,657,324, the number _____ is in the ones place.

6. In 8,158,760, the number _____ is in the millions place.

7. In 9,708,165, the number _____ is in the ten thousands place.

Place Value

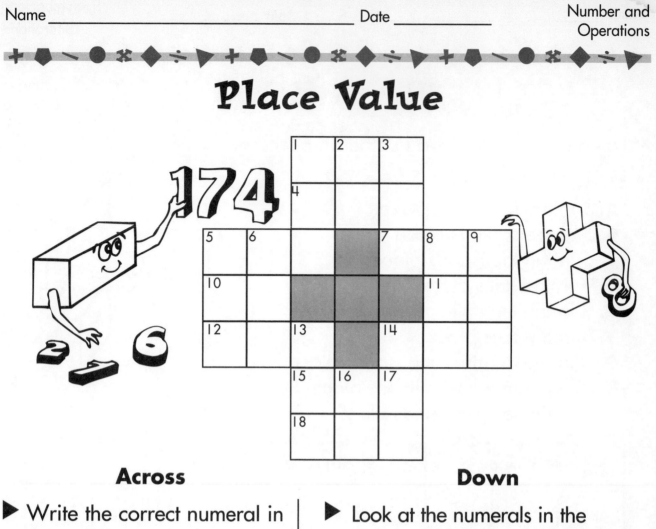

Across

▶ Write the correct numeral in the puzzle.

1. seven hundred fifty-one

4. two hundred eighty-five

5. nine hundred eight

7. six hundred seventy-eight

10. sixty-five

11. eighty-three

12. seven hundred forty-one

14. two hundred fifty-seven

15. five hundred twenty-three

18. four hundred ninety-five

Down

▶ Look at the numerals in the puzzle to write the missing words.

1. _____ hundred twenty- _____

2. _____-eight

3. _____ hundred _____

5. nine _____ sixty-_____

6. fifty-_____

8. _____ hundred _____ five

9. eight hundred _____

13. _____ hundred _____

14. two hundred _____

16. _____

Rounding

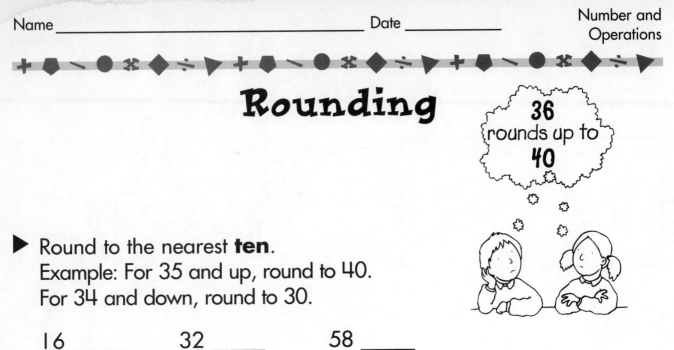

36
rounds up to
40

▶ Round to the nearest **ten**.
Example: For 35 and up, round to 40.
For 34 and down, round to 30.

16 _____	32 _____	58 _____
75 _____	92 _____	82 _____
27 _____	54 _____	66 _____

▶ Round to the nearest **hundred**.
Example: For 350 and up, round to 400.
For 349 and down, round to 300.

921 _____	662 _____	882 _____
458 _____	187 _____	363 _____
393 _____	527 _____	211 _____

▶ Round to nearest **thousand**.
Example: For 6,500 and up, round to 7,000.
For 6,499 and down, round to 6,000.

2,495 _____	3,379 _____	4,289 _____
7,001 _____	8,821 _____	6,213 _____
5,111 _____	9,339 _____	2,985 _____

Addition

Add ones.	Add tens.
46 + 21 7	46 + 21 67

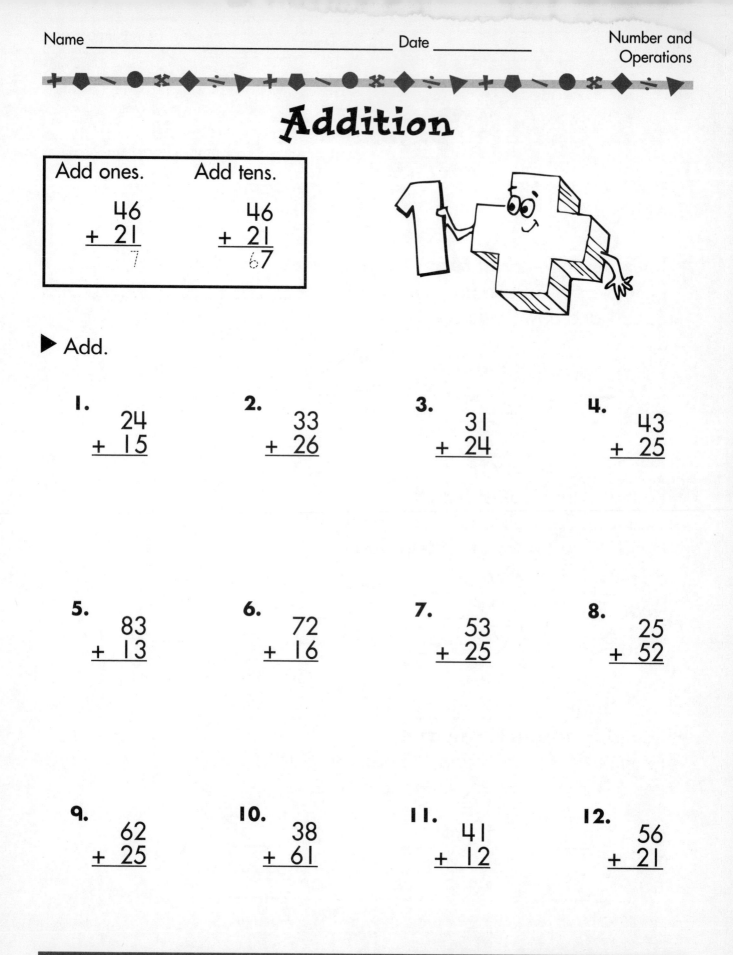

▶ Add.

1.
```
   24
 + 15
```

2.
```
   33
 + 26
```

3.
```
   31
 + 24
```

4.
```
   43
 + 25
```

5.
```
   83
 + 13
```

6.
```
   72
 + 16
```

7.
```
   53
 + 25
```

8.
```
   25
 + 52
```

9.
```
   62
 + 25
```

10.
```
   38
 + 61
```

11.
```
   41
 + 12
```

12.
```
   56
 + 21
```

Addition

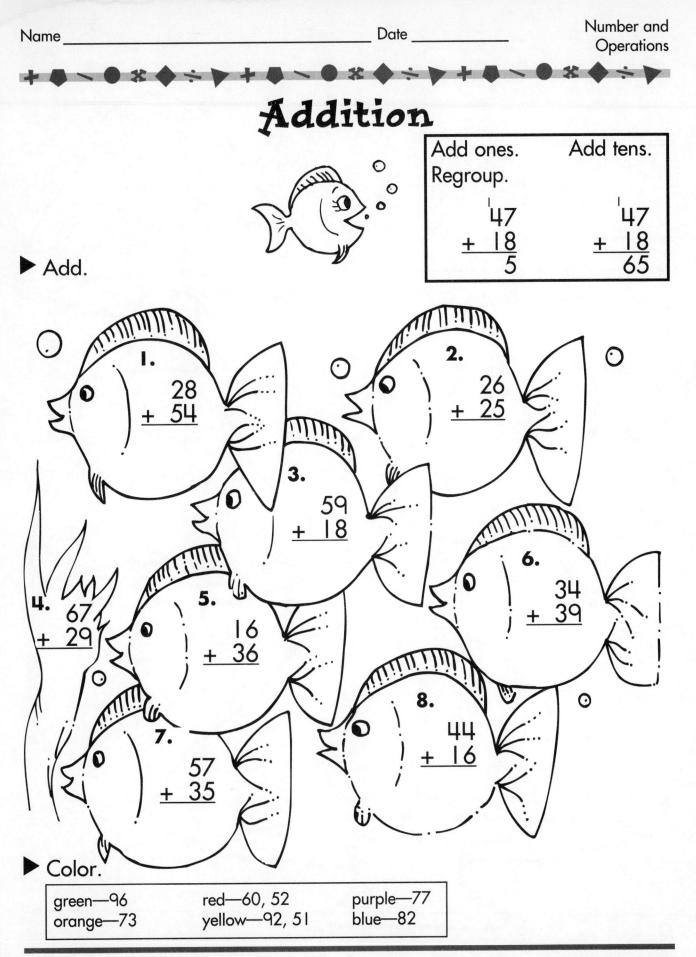

Add ones. Regroup.	Add tens.
$\begin{array}{r} ^{1}47 \\ +\ 18 \\ \hline 5 \end{array}$	$\begin{array}{r} ^{1}47 \\ +\ 18 \\ \hline 65 \end{array}$

▶ Add.

1. $\begin{array}{r} 28 \\ +\ 54 \\ \hline \end{array}$

2. $\begin{array}{r} 26 \\ +\ 25 \\ \hline \end{array}$

3. $\begin{array}{r} 59 \\ +\ 18 \\ \hline \end{array}$

4. $\begin{array}{r} 67 \\ +\ 29 \\ \hline \end{array}$

5. $\begin{array}{r} 16 \\ +\ 36 \\ \hline \end{array}$

6. $\begin{array}{r} 34 \\ +\ 39 \\ \hline \end{array}$

7. $\begin{array}{r} 57 \\ +\ 35 \\ \hline \end{array}$

8. $\begin{array}{r} 44 \\ +\ 16 \\ \hline \end{array}$

▶ Color.

green—96	red—60, 52	purple—77
orange—73	yellow—92, 51	blue—82

0-7424-1721-2 Math

Addition

Add.   52 + 28 = 80
        28 + 91 = 119
        119 + 80 = ?

▶ Follow arrows to complete the
addition mushrooms.

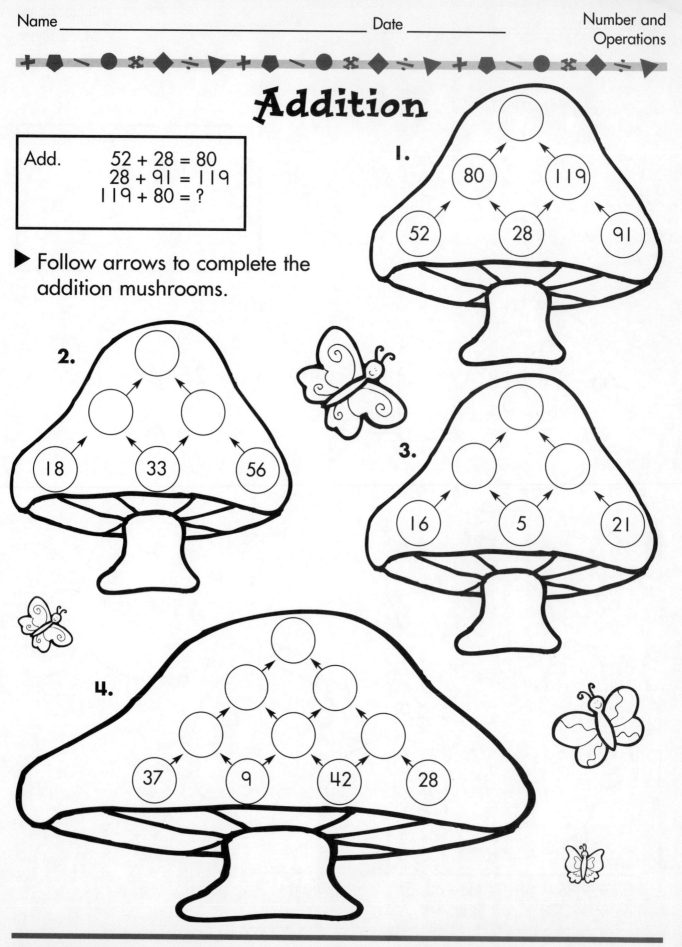

Addition

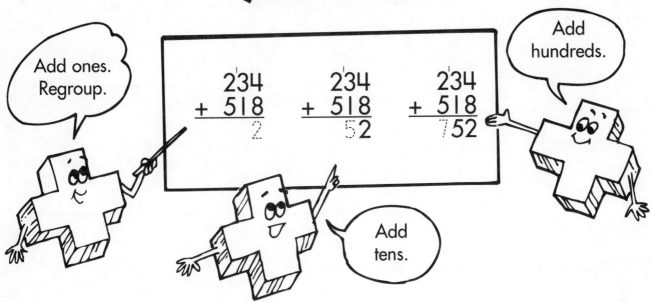

▶ Add.

1.
  362
+ 119

2.
  428
+ 358

3.
  524
+ 167

4.
  665
+ 219

5.
  767
+ 213

6.
  818
+ 169

7.
  136
+ 255

8.
  345
+ 527

9.
  677
+ 116

10.
  526
+ 318

11.
  727
+ 267

12.
  634
+ 158

Addition

Add ones.	Add tens. Regroup.	Add hundreds.
345 + 271 6	345 + 271 16	345 + 271 616

▶ What do you call a bull that's asleep?

836	756	637	545	719	777	728	749	409
L	O	U	D	A	B	R	E	Z

▶ Add. Then use the code to answer the riddle.

563 + 156	484 + 293	256 + 381	595 + 241	352 + 484

254 + 291	375 + 381	285 + 124	558 + 191	466 + 262

Addition

▶ Help the ant get to the picnic. Complete the problems and shade
each box that has a 9 in the answer.

836 + 90	536 + 248	952 + 8	362 + 47	486 + 293
789 526 + 214	2,846 + 6,478	932 + 365	374 + 299	956 874 + 65
4,768 + 2,894	38 456 + 3,894	4,507 + 2,743	404 + 289	1,843 + 6,752
639 + 77	587 342 + 679	5,379 1,865 + 2,348	450 + 145	594 + 278
29 875 + 2,341	387 29 + 5,614	462 379 + 248		

Addition

$$
\begin{array}{r} 38 \\ 45 \\ +29 \\ \hline \end{array}
$$

$$
\begin{array}{r} ^{2}38 \\ 45 \\ +\ 29 \\ \hline 2 \end{array}
\qquad
\begin{array}{r} 13 \\ +\ \ 9 \\ \hline 22 \end{array}
\qquad
\begin{array}{r} 5 \\ +\ 4 \\ \hline 9 \end{array}
\qquad
\begin{array}{r} 9 \\ +\ 2 \\ \hline 11 \end{array}
\qquad
\begin{array}{r} ^{2}38 \\ 45 \\ +\ 29 \\ \hline 112 \end{array}
$$

▶ Add.

1.
$$
\begin{array}{r} 38 \\ 25 \\ +\ 63 \\ \hline \end{array}
$$

2.
$$
\begin{array}{r} 51 \\ 49 \\ +\ 73 \\ \hline \end{array}
$$

3.
$$
\begin{array}{r} 92 \\ 29 \\ +\ 64 \\ \hline \end{array}
$$

4.
$$
\begin{array}{r} 85 \\ 27 \\ +\ 78 \\ \hline \end{array}
$$

5.
$$
\begin{array}{r} 98 \\ 89 \\ +\ 76 \\ \hline \end{array}
$$

6.
$$
\begin{array}{r} 67 \\ 28 \\ +\ 87 \\ \hline \end{array}
$$

7.
$$
\begin{array}{r} 96 \\ 79 \\ +\ 68 \\ \hline \end{array}
$$

8.
$$
\begin{array}{r} 49 \\ 96 \\ +\ 58 \\ \hline \end{array}
$$

9.
$$
\begin{array}{r} 33 \\ 44 \\ +\ 66 \\ \hline \end{array}
$$

10.
$$
\begin{array}{r} 61 \\ 93 \\ +\ 87 \\ \hline \end{array}
$$

11.
$$
\begin{array}{r} 54 \\ 88 \\ +\ 73 \\ \hline \end{array}
$$

12.
$$
\begin{array}{r} 52 \\ 16 \\ 13 \\ +\ 52 \\ \hline \end{array}
$$

Addition Problem Solving

▶ Macy's mom works at a music store. Macy helped her mom keep track of CDs at the store. Write the answer to each problem on the line.

1. There are 762 CD titles listed in the computer. Macy enters 292 new titles into the computer. What is the total number of CD titles listed now? _____

2. One day, 278 CDs were sold. The next day, 183 CDs were sold. What is the total number of CDs sold in those two days? _____

3. The music store had 757 customers last month and 662 customers this month. How many customers did the store have all together in those two months? _____

▶ Todd's mom has a special plan for his birthday. Write the answer to each problem on the line.

4. Todd's mom took him and a friend to a water park for his birthday. His friend, Steve, walked 3 blocks to get to Todd's house. Then Todd, his mom, and Steve walked 6 more blocks to the water park. How many blocks did Steve walk by the time he got back home later that night? _____

5. Mom, Todd, and Steve were standing in line at the ticket counter. There were 8 people standing in front of them and 4 people standing behind them. How many people were standing in line? _____

6. An adult ticket costs $12.00. A child's ticket costs half that much. Todd and Steve are charged the child's ticket price. How much did Mom pay for the tickets to the water park? Write how you would find the answer to this problem.

_____

_____

Subtraction

Regroup. (1 ten = 10 ones)	Subtract ones.	Subtract tens.
$\begin{array}{r} ^4\cancel{5}{}^1 8 \\ -\ 2\ 9 \\ \hline \end{array}$	$\begin{array}{r} ^4\cancel{5}{}^1 8 \\ -\ 2\ 9 \\ \hline 9 \end{array}$	$\begin{array}{r} ^4\cancel{5}{}^1 8 \\ -\ 2\ 9 \\ \hline 2\ 9 \end{array}$

▶ Subtract.

1.
$$\begin{array}{r} 96 \\ -\ 27 \\ \hline \end{array}$$

2.
$$\begin{array}{r} 35 \\ -\ 19 \\ \hline \end{array}$$

3.
$$\begin{array}{r} 87 \\ -\ 68 \\ \hline \end{array}$$

4.
$$\begin{array}{r} 45 \\ -\ 18 \\ \hline \end{array}$$

5.
$$\begin{array}{r} 31 \\ -\ 19 \\ \hline \end{array}$$

6.
$$\begin{array}{r} 86 \\ -\ 58 \\ \hline \end{array}$$

7.
$$\begin{array}{r} 67 \\ -\ 29 \\ \hline \end{array}$$

8.
$$\begin{array}{r} 73 \\ -\ 29 \\ \hline \end{array}$$

9.
$$\begin{array}{r} 55 \\ -\ 27 \\ \hline \end{array}$$

10.
$$\begin{array}{r} 81 \\ -\ 69 \\ \hline \end{array}$$

11.
$$\begin{array}{r} 63 \\ -\ 17 \\ \hline \end{array}$$

12.
$$\begin{array}{r} 98 \\ -\ 19 \\ \hline \end{array}$$

Subtraction

▶ As you complete the problems, mark off the numbers on the MATHO cards below to discover the winning card.

M A T H O

177	413	127	149	939
13	346	167	25	174
513	89	Free	49	208
38	186	218	74	139
575	438	91	158	22

M A T H O

58	83	95	179	414
919	405	719	819	274
616	69	Free	601	272
374	211	116	27	424
143	79	101	81	35

M A T H O

259	42	339	520	225
91	28	511	625	871
582	39	Free	81	22
52	63	464	19	70
365	91	616	128	138

1.
```
   92
 - 54
```

2.
```
  126
 - 77
```

3.
```
  192
 - 49
```

4.
```
   71
 - 46
```

5.
```
  317
 - 58
```

6.
```
  452
 - 47
```

7.
```
  260
 - 49
```

8.
```
   98
 - 29
```

9.
```
  265
 - 79
```

10.
```
  121
 - 82
```

11.
```
  883
 - 64
```

12.
```
  974
 - 35
```

13.
```
  147
 - 84
```

14.
```
  174
 - 58
```

15.
```
  483
 - 69
```

Subtraction

10 ⟷ 111111

Regroup. (1 ten = 10 ones)	Subtract ones.	Regroup. (1 hundred = 10 tens)	Subtract tens.	Subtract hundreds.
$\begin{array}{r} 8\overset{6}{\cancel{7}}\overset{1}{4} \\ -\ 388 \\ \hline \end{array}$	$\begin{array}{r} 8\overset{6}{\cancel{7}}\overset{1}{4} \\ -\ 388 \\ \hline 6 \end{array}$	$\begin{array}{r} \overset{7}{\cancel{8}}\overset{16}{\cancel{7}}\overset{1}{4} \\ -\ 388 \\ \hline 6 \end{array}$	$\begin{array}{r} \overset{7}{\cancel{8}}\overset{16}{\cancel{7}}\overset{1}{4} \\ -\ 388 \\ \hline 86 \end{array}$	$\begin{array}{r} \overset{7}{\cancel{8}}\overset{16}{\cancel{7}}\overset{1}{4} \\ -\ 388 \\ \hline 486 \end{array}$

► Subtract.

1. $\begin{array}{r} 746 \\ -\ 278 \\ \hline \end{array}$

2. $\begin{array}{r} 654 \\ -\ 285 \\ \hline \end{array}$

3. $\begin{array}{r} 942 \\ -\ 678 \\ \hline \end{array}$

4. $\begin{array}{r} 827 \\ -\ 139 \\ \hline \end{array}$

5. $\begin{array}{r} 467 \\ -\ 378 \\ \hline \end{array}$

6. $\begin{array}{r} 747 \\ -\ 598 \\ \hline \end{array}$

7. $\begin{array}{r} 663 \\ -\ 177 \\ \hline \end{array}$

8. $\begin{array}{r} 542 \\ -\ 276 \\ \hline \end{array}$

9. $\begin{array}{r} 311 \\ -\ 127 \\ \hline \end{array}$

10. $\begin{array}{r} 422 \\ -\ 158 \\ \hline \end{array}$

11. $\begin{array}{r} 535 \\ -\ 348 \\ \hline \end{array}$

12. $\begin{array}{r} 723 \\ -\ 158 \\ \hline \end{array}$

Subtraction

Subtract ones.	Regroup. (1 hundred = 10 tens)	Subtract tens.	Subtract hundreds.

537
− 185
    2
	$\overset{4}{\cancel{5}}\overset{1}{3}7$
	− 185
	      2
		$\overset{4}{\cancel{5}}\overset{1}{3}7$
		− 185
		    5 2
			$\overset{4}{\cancel{5}}\overset{1}{3}7$
			− 185
			  3 5 2

▶ Subtract.

1.   918
   − 652

2.   738
   − 284

3.   628
   − 231

4.   437
   − 175

5.   758
   − 364

6.   878
   − 690

7.   532
   − 41

8.   425
   − 362

9.   735
   − 462

10. 989
   − 296

11. 547
   − 266

12. 827
   − 382

0-7424-1721-2 Math

Subtraction

▶ Work problems and use the code to answer the riddle.

1.	2.	3.	4.
623 − 458	935 − 567	824 − 168	423 − 267

5.	6.	7.	8.
986 − 197	815 − 159	852 − 696	546 − 197

9.	10.	11.	12.
934 − 769	564 − 287	321 − 157	725 − 536

▶ What has four legs and flies?

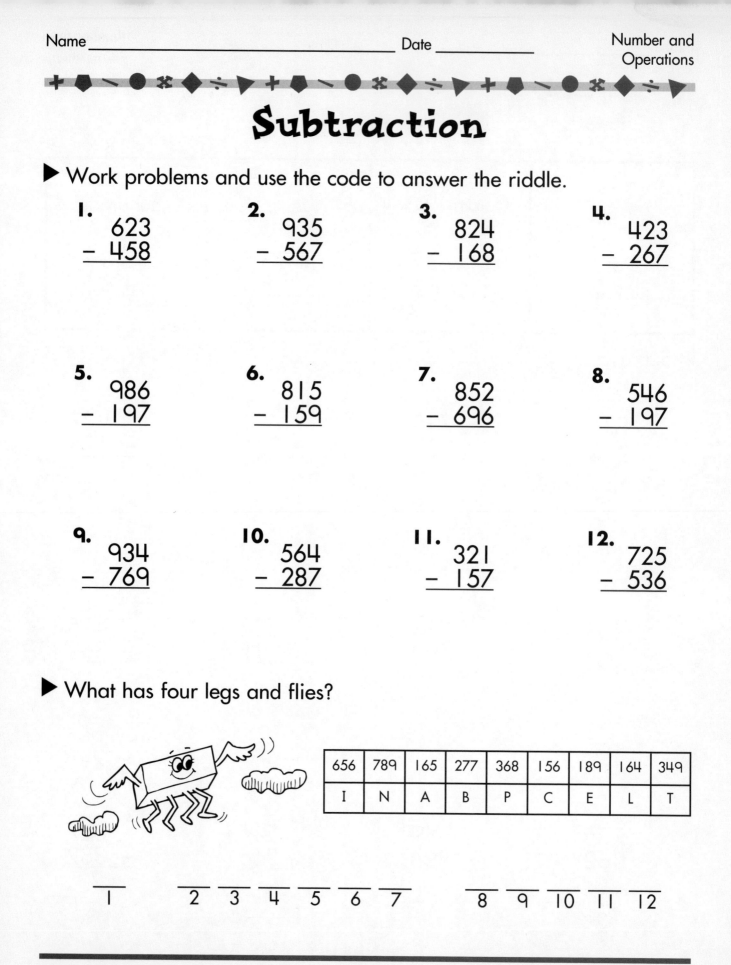

656	789	165	277	368	156	189	164	349
I	N	A	B	P	C	E	L	T

‾1‾ ‾2‾ ‾3‾ ‾4‾ ‾5‾ ‾6‾ ‾7‾ ‾8‾ ‾9‾ ‾10‾ ‾11‾ ‾12‾

Subtraction

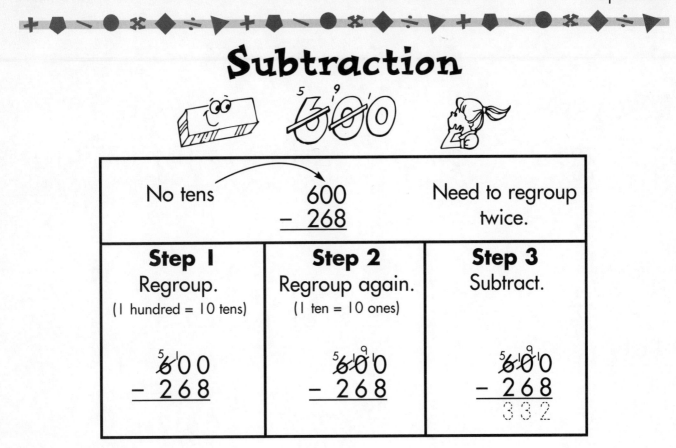

No tens	$\begin{array}{r} 600 \\ -\ 268 \end{array}$	Need to regroup twice.

Step 1 Regroup. (1 hundred = 10 tens)	**Step 2** Regroup again. (1 ten = 10 ones)	**Step 3** Subtract.
$\begin{array}{r} \overset{5}{6}\overset{1}{0}0 \\ -\ 2\,6\,8 \end{array}$	$\begin{array}{r} \overset{5}{6}\overset{1\,9}{0}0 \\ -\ 2\,6\,8 \end{array}$	$\begin{array}{r} \overset{5}{6}\overset{1\,9}{0}0 \\ -\ 2\,6\,8 \\ \hline 3\,3\,2 \end{array}$

▶ Subtract.

1. $\begin{array}{r} 800 \\ -\ 567 \\ \hline \end{array}$

2. $\begin{array}{r} 505 \\ -\ 289 \\ \hline \end{array}$

3. $\begin{array}{r} 603 \\ -\ 185 \\ \hline \end{array}$

4. $\begin{array}{r} 401 \\ -\ 289 \\ \hline \end{array}$

5. $\begin{array}{r} 308 \\ -\ 179 \\ \hline \end{array}$

6. $\begin{array}{r} 700 \\ -\ 207 \\ \hline \end{array}$

7. $\begin{array}{r} 500 \\ -\ 236 \\ \hline \end{array}$

8. $\begin{array}{r} 608 \\ -\ 248 \\ \hline \end{array}$

9. $\begin{array}{r} 807 \\ -\ 658 \\ \hline \end{array}$

10. $\begin{array}{r} 947 \\ -\ 509 \\ \hline \end{array}$

11. $\begin{array}{r} 400 \\ -\ 298 \\ \hline \end{array}$

12. $\begin{array}{r} 702 \\ -\ 537 \\ \hline \end{array}$

Subtraction

▶ Work problems.

1.
```
  6,723
- 2,586
```

2.
```
   547
-  259
```

3.
```
   834
-  463
```

4.
```
  7,146
- 3,498
```

5.
```
  9,427
- 6,648
```

6.
```
  8,149
- 5,372
```

7.
```
   421
-  275
```

8.
```
  7,456
- 3,724
```

9.
```
   818
-  639
```

10.
```
   772
-  586
```

11.
```
  6,529
- 4,538
```

12.
```
  5,379
- 2,835
```

13.
```
  6,275
- 3,761
```

14.
```
  5,612
- 1,505
```

▶ Shade in answers to find path.

2,514	288	186	3,732	4,107
2,779	156	1,901	2,414	4,137
3,748	3,337	2,777	371	179	1,991
3,048	3,737	146	2,717		
679	237	2,544	3,648		

Over here!

Subtraction Problem Solving

▶ Ms. Ramon's gym class is practicing for the Fitness Challenge. There are two teams with four students on each team. To complete the challenge, each team must complete the following exercises:

100	sit-ups
100	push-ups
120	jumping jacks
2,000	meters of running

▶ Fill in the totals for the tables below. Then answer the questions.

Team 1

Student	Sit-Ups	Push-Ups	Jumping Jacks	Meters Run
Mariana	24	21	23	300
Jacob	17	18	25	500
Carlos	25	23	18	250
Emily	25	20	17	450
Team Total				

Team 2

Student	Sit-Ups	Push-Ups	Jumping Jacks	Meters Run
Samuel	25	24	17	300
Natalie	18	19	25	500
Jonah	21	16	25	450
Kanesha	18	25	21	500
Team Total				

1. How many push-ups does team one have to do to finish the contest? _____

2. What is the total number of jumping jacks remaining for team two? _____

3. Which team has the most sit-ups left to do? _____

4. Which team has the least number of meters left to run? _____

Multiplication

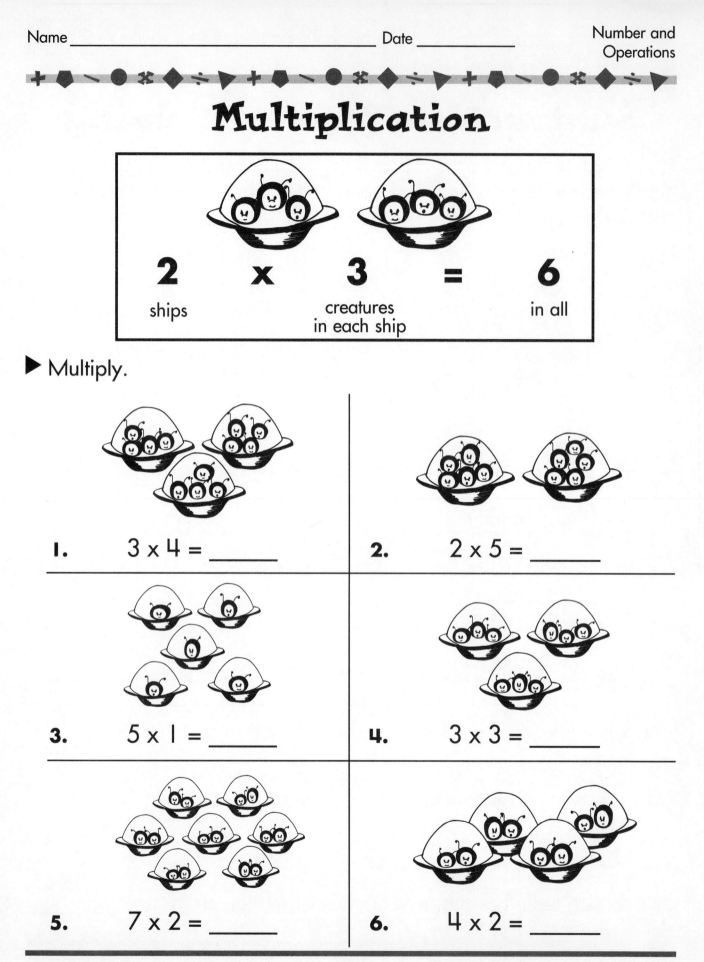

2 x **3** = **6**

ships   creatures in each ship   in all

▶ Multiply.

1. $3 \times 4 =$ _____

2. $2 \times 5 =$ _____

3. $5 \times 1 =$ _____

4. $3 \times 3 =$ _____

5. $7 \times 2 =$ _____

6. $4 \times 2 =$ _____

Multiplication

▶ Multiply.

1. 6 x 9	**2.** 5 x 3	**3.** 8 x 6	**4.** 9 x 2
5. 7 x 6	**6.** 5 x 6	**7.** 8 x 3	**8.** 9 x 8
9. 4 x 4	**10.** 4 x 6	**11.** 8 x 7	**12.** 7 x 4
13. 8 x 2	**14.** 5 x 5	**15.** 7 x 9	**16.** 9 x 3

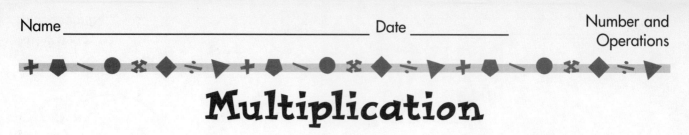

Multiplication

▶ Fill in the table. Can you do it in less than three minutes?

x	0	1	2	3	4	5	6	7	8	9
0										
1										
2			4							
3										
4										
5						25				
6										
7										
8										
9										

Multiplication

$$\frac{\times 3}{12} \qquad \frac{\times 4}{12}$$

▶ If you change the order of the factors, you have the same product.

1. $7 \times 3 =$ _____   2. $6 \times 5 =$ _____

    $3 \times 7 =$ _____ $5 \times 6 =$ _____

3. $2 \times 3 =$ _____   4. $4 \times 6 =$ _____

    $3 \times 2 =$ _____ $6 \times 4 =$ _____

5. $2 \times 9 =$ _____   6. $8 \times 4 =$ _____

    $9 \times 2 =$ _____ $4 \times 8 =$ _____

7. $7 \times 2 =$ _____   8. $3 \times 6 =$ _____

    $2 \times 7 =$ _____ $6 \times 3 =$ _____

9. $9 \times 4 =$ _____   10. $8 \times 3 =$ _____

    $4 \times 9 =$ _____ $3 \times 8 =$ _____

11. $5 \times 2 =$ _____   12. $9 \times 3 =$ _____

    $2 \times 5 =$ _____ $3 \times 9 =$ _____

Multiplication

▶ Multiply.

1.
$$\begin{array}{r} 5 \\ \times\ 5 \\ \hline \end{array}$$

2.
$$\begin{array}{r} 7 \\ \times\ 3 \\ \hline \end{array}$$

3.
$$\begin{array}{r} 2 \\ \times\ 9 \\ \hline \end{array}$$

4.
$$\begin{array}{r} 7 \\ \times\ 8 \\ \hline \end{array}$$

5.
$$\begin{array}{r} 9 \\ \times\ 7 \\ \hline \end{array}$$

6.
$$\begin{array}{r} 6 \\ \times\ 6 \\ \hline \end{array}$$

7.
$$\begin{array}{r} 9 \\ \times\ 5 \\ \hline \end{array}$$

8.
$$\begin{array}{r} 6 \\ \times\ 7 \\ \hline \end{array}$$

9.
$$\begin{array}{r} 2 \\ \times\ 5 \\ \hline \end{array}$$

10.
$$\begin{array}{r} 5 \\ \times\ 7 \\ \hline \end{array}$$

11.
$$\begin{array}{r} 9 \\ \times\ 9 \\ \hline \end{array}$$

12.
$$\begin{array}{r} 8 \\ \times\ 5 \\ \hline \end{array}$$

13.
$$\begin{array}{r} 6 \\ \times\ 5 \\ \hline \end{array}$$

14.
$$\begin{array}{r} 9 \\ \times\ 8 \\ \hline \end{array}$$

15.
$$\begin{array}{r} 3 \\ \times\ 8 \\ \hline \end{array}$$

16.
$$\begin{array}{r} 4 \\ \times\ 7 \\ \hline \end{array}$$

Multiplication

$$
\begin{array}{r} 65 \\ \times\ 24 \\ \hline \end{array}
\qquad
\begin{array}{r} {}^{2}65 \\ \times\ 24 \\ \hline 260 \end{array}
\qquad
\begin{array}{r} {}^{1}\,{}^{2}65 \\ \times\ 24 \\ \hline 260 \\ 130 \\ \hline \end{array}
\qquad
\begin{array}{r} {}^{1}\,{}^{2}65 \\ \times\ 24 \\ \hline 260 \\ 130 \\ \hline 1,560 \end{array}
$$

▶ Multiply.

1.
$$\begin{array}{r} 11 \\ \times\ 54 \\ \hline \end{array}$$

2.
$$\begin{array}{r} 28 \\ \times\ 11 \\ \hline \end{array}$$

3.
$$\begin{array}{r} 65 \\ \times\ 22 \\ \hline \end{array}$$

4.
$$\begin{array}{r} 19 \\ \times\ 49 \\ \hline \end{array}$$

5.
$$\begin{array}{r} 98 \\ \times\ 12 \\ \hline \end{array}$$

6.
$$\begin{array}{r} 36 \\ \times\ 15 \\ \hline \end{array}$$

7.
$$\begin{array}{r} 42 \\ \times\ 25 \\ \hline \end{array}$$

8.
$$\begin{array}{r} 19 \\ \times\ 37 \\ \hline \end{array}$$

9.
$$\begin{array}{r} 49 \\ \times\ 38 \\ \hline \end{array}$$

10.
$$\begin{array}{r} 19 \\ \times\ 48 \\ \hline \end{array}$$

11.
$$\begin{array}{r} 56 \\ \times\ 61 \\ \hline \end{array}$$

12.
$$\begin{array}{r} 45 \\ \times\ 32 \\ \hline \end{array}$$

13.
$$\begin{array}{r} 37 \\ \times\ 84 \\ \hline \end{array}$$

14.
$$\begin{array}{r} 68 \\ \times\ 98 \\ \hline \end{array}$$

15.
$$\begin{array}{r} 28 \\ \times\ 85 \\ \hline \end{array}$$

Multiplication

▶ Multiply target center by next row to get outer row answer. Add all answers from outer row to get target total. Can you find the winning dartboard with the most points?

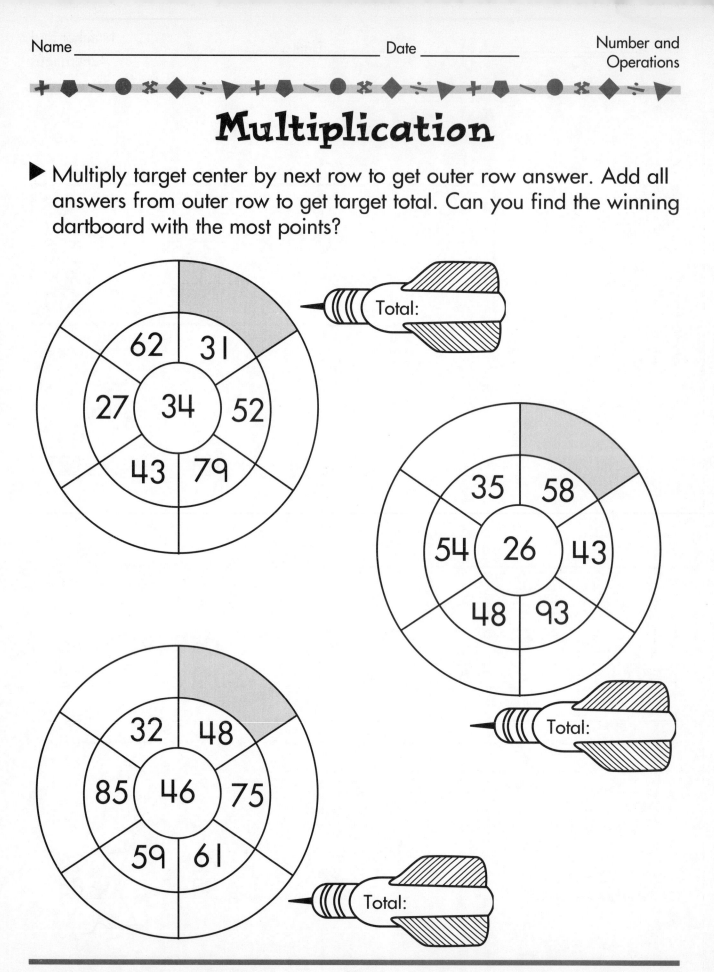

Multiplication

▶ Work problems. Use code to find "GREAT" in each language.

Row 1 — Swahili

1.	2.	3.	4.	5.
367 x 88	211 x 26	744 x 75	861 x 44	524 x 38
_____	_____	_____	_____	_____

Row 2 — Dutch

6.	7.	8.	9.	10.
682 x 95	553 x 64	724 x 49	648 x 89	472 x 84
_____	_____	_____	_____	_____

Row 3 — Spanish

11.	12.	13.	14.	15.
351 x 65	438 x 95	942 x 72	313 x 78	946 x 48
_____	_____	_____	_____	_____

5,486 = J	35,392 = O	45,408 = O
19,912 = U	35,476 = E	55,800 = A
22,815 = B	37,884 = B	57,672 = D
24,414 = N	39,648 = !	64,790 = G
32,296 = A	41,610 = U	67,824 = E

GREAT!
English

Multiplication Problem Solving

▶ The students at P.S. 134 are having a book sale. They are arranging the books into categories and stacking them on tables. Read the following problems and write your answer on the line. Use what you know about multiplication to solve the problems.

1. Josh sorted books about sports. When he was finished, he had 8 stacks of 6 books each. How many sports books in all were at the sale?

_____

2. The largest category of books was fiction. Rebecca had 12 stacks with 10 books in each stack. How many fiction books were at the sale?

_____

3. The book sale was in the gym. The students set up tables into 9 rows with 4 tables in each row. What was the total number of tables in the gym?

_____

4. The customers were excited by the sale. They lined up to pay for their books. There were 5 lines with 17 customers in each line. How many customers were waiting to pay?

_____

5. The table with picture books for children was a mess. Hee-Jung sorted them into stacks. When she was finished, she had 12 stacks with 5 books in each stack. How many picture books were there at the sale?

_____

6. When the sale was over, the students counted the money. Bruno counted the five-dollar bills. He had 14 five-dollar bills. How much money did Bruno have?

_____

Division

▶ Arrange jersey digits in the footballs to get the correct answer.

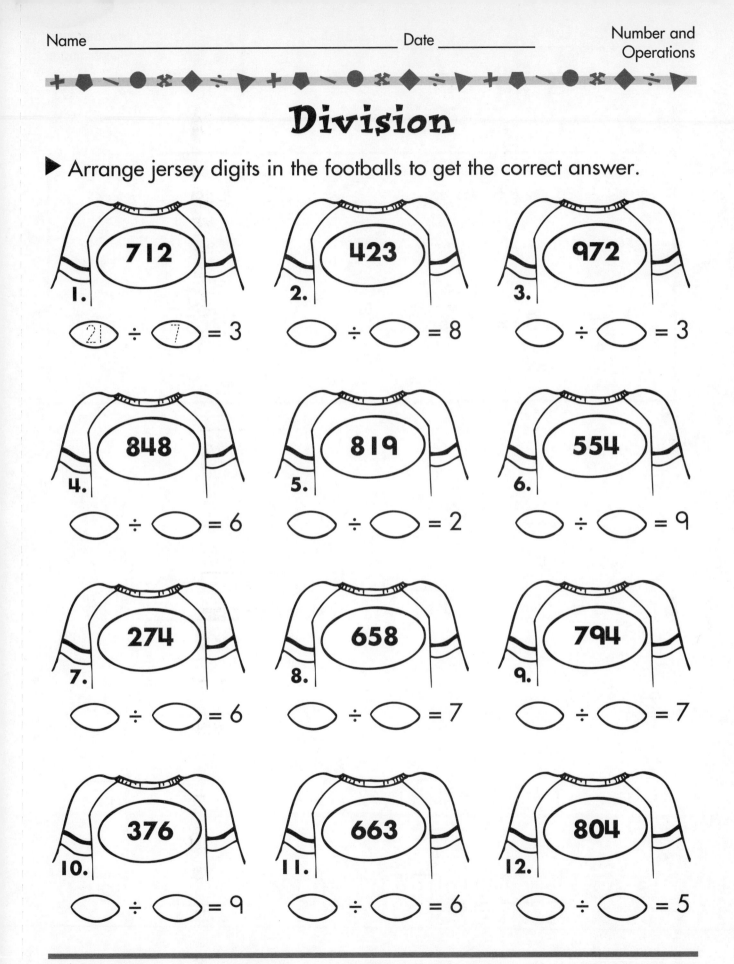

1. **712**   ⬭2⬭ ÷ ⬭7⬭ = 3

2. **423**   ◯ ÷ ◯ = 8

3. **972**   ◯ ÷ ◯ = 3

4. **848**   ◯ ÷ ◯ = 6

5. **819**   ◯ ÷ ◯ = 2

6. **554**   ◯ ÷ ◯ = 9

7. **274**   ◯ ÷ ◯ = 6

8. **658**   ◯ ÷ ◯ = 7

9. **794**   ◯ ÷ ◯ = 7

10. **376**   ◯ ÷ ◯ = 9

11. **663**   ◯ ÷ ◯ = 6

12. **804**   ◯ ÷ ◯ = 5

Division

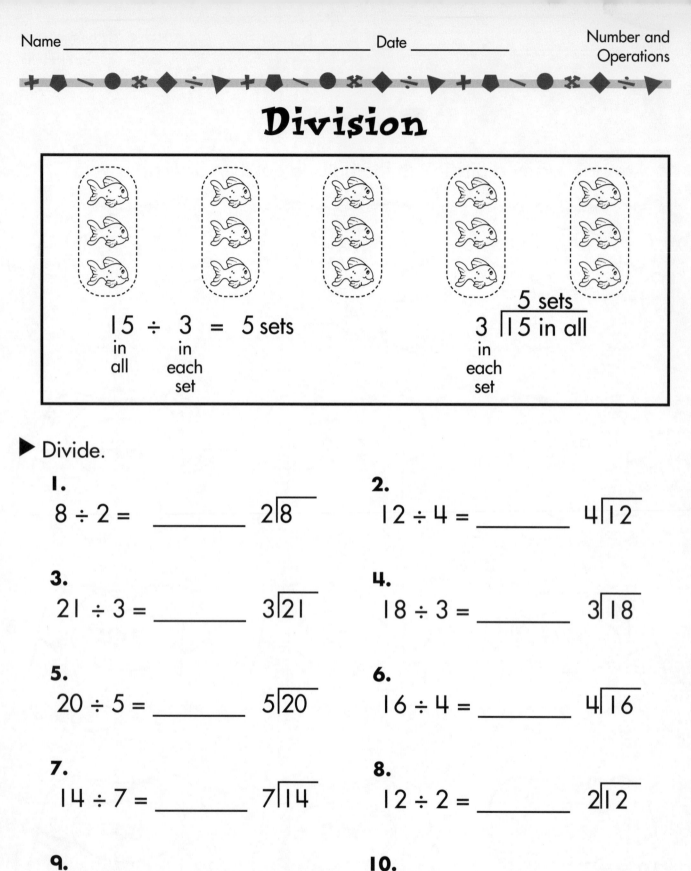

$15 \div 3 = 5$ sets
in all   in each set

$3\overline{)15}$ 5 sets
in all
in each set

▶ Divide.

1.

$8 \div 2 =$ _____ $2\overline{)8}$

2.

$12 \div 4 =$ _____ $4\overline{)12}$

3.

$21 \div 3 =$ _____ $3\overline{)21}$

4.

$18 \div 3 =$ _____ $3\overline{)18}$

5.

$20 \div 5 =$ _____ $5\overline{)20}$

6.

$16 \div 4 =$ _____ $4\overline{)16}$

7.

$14 \div 7 =$ _____ $7\overline{)14}$

8.

$12 \div 2 =$ _____ $2\overline{)12}$

9.

$18 \div 2 =$ _____ $2\overline{)18}$

10.

$24 \div 6 =$ _____ $6\overline{)24}$

Division

9, 7, 5, 3 = X

8, 6, 4, 2 = 0

X wins _____ times.
0 wins _____ times.

▶ X on odd answers. O on even answers.

$4\overline{)36}$	$4\overline{)24}$	$10 \div 5$	$24 \div 4$	$5\overline{)45}$	$28 \div 4$
$5\overline{)40}$	$32 \div 4$	$25 \div 5$	$4\overline{)36}$	$5\overline{)20}$	$8 \div 4$
$35 \div 5$	$20 \div 4$	$12 \div 4$	$4\overline{)16}$	$5\overline{)15}$	$30 \div 5$

$5\overline{)10}$	$4\overline{)8}$	$24 \div 4$
$4\overline{)36}$	$5\overline{)35}$	$4\overline{)32}$
$45 \div 5$	$5\overline{)30}$	$4\overline{)12}$

$4\overline{)12}$	$5\overline{)10}$	$5\overline{)45}$	$28 \div 4$	$5\overline{)30}$	$45 \div 5$
$30 \div 5$	$5\overline{)25}$	$35 \div 5$	$16 \div 4$	$32 \div 4$	$15 \div 5$
$4\overline{)32}$	$8 \div 4$	$5\overline{)20}$	$4\overline{)20}$	$4\overline{)12}$	$21\overline{)7}$

Division

Use me when a problem doesn't come out even.

$$
\begin{array}{r}
6 \\
4\overline{)22}
\end{array}
$$
No Remainder
6 is too many.

$$
\begin{array}{r}
5\,R2 \\
4\overline{)22} \\
-20 \\
\hline
2
\end{array}
$$
Remainder

▶ Divide.

1. $5\overline{)28}$ 5 R

2. $4\overline{)19}$ 4 R

3. $8\overline{)26}$ 3 R

4. $7\overline{)45}$ 6 R

5. $3\overline{)26}$ R

6. $2\overline{)19}$ R

7. $6\overline{)51}$ R

8. $9\overline{)65}$ R

9. $8\overline{)43}$ R

10. $9\overline{)59}$ R

11. $7\overline{)33}$ R

12. $4\overline{)27}$ R

Name _____ Date _____

Number and
Operations

Division

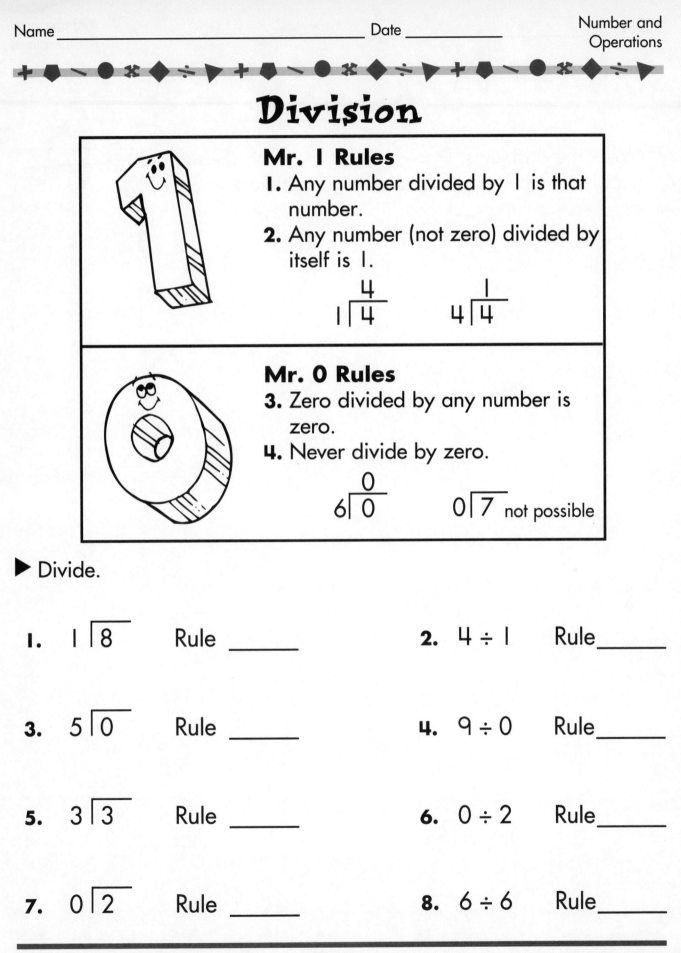

Mr. 1 Rules

1. Any number divided by 1 is that number.
2. Any number (not zero) divided by itself is 1.

$$1\overline{)4} = 4 \qquad 4\overline{)4} = 1$$

Mr. 0 Rules

3. Zero divided by any number is zero.
4. Never divide by zero.

$$6\overline{)0} = 0 \qquad 0\overline{)7} \text{ not possible}$$

▶ Divide.

1. $1\overline{)8}$ Rule _____

2. $4 \div 1$ Rule _____

3. $5\overline{)0}$ Rule _____

4. $9 \div 0$ Rule _____

5. $3\overline{)3}$ Rule _____

6. $0 \div 2$ Rule _____

7. $0\overline{)2}$ Rule _____

8. $6 \div 6$ Rule _____

Division

▶ Work the problems. Draw a line from each division
problem to the matching checking problem.

1. 3⟌56

2. 3⟌64

3. 3⟌276

4. 3⟌127

5. 3⟌178

6. 3⟌175

7. 3⟌236

8. 3⟌32

9. 3⟌86

10. 3⟌247

$$\begin{array}{r} 92 \\ \times\ 3 \\ \hline \end{array}$$

$$\begin{array}{r} 59 \\ \times\ 3 \\ \hline \end{array}$$

$$\begin{array}{r} 21 \\ \times\ 3 \\ \hline \end{array}$$

$$\begin{array}{r} 42 \\ \times\ 3 \\ \hline \end{array}$$

$$\begin{array}{r} 18 \\ \times\ 3 \\ \hline \end{array}$$

$$\begin{array}{r} 10 \\ \times\ 3 \\ \hline \end{array}$$

$$\begin{array}{r} 58 \\ \times\ 3 \\ \hline \end{array}$$

$$\begin{array}{r} 28 \\ \times\ 3 \\ \hline \end{array}$$

$$\begin{array}{r} 78 \\ \times\ 3 \\ \hline \end{array}$$

$$\begin{array}{r} 82 \\ \times\ 3 \\ \hline \end{array}$$

Division

▶ Work the problems inside the cocoons. Then draw a line to the
butterfly with the correct answer.

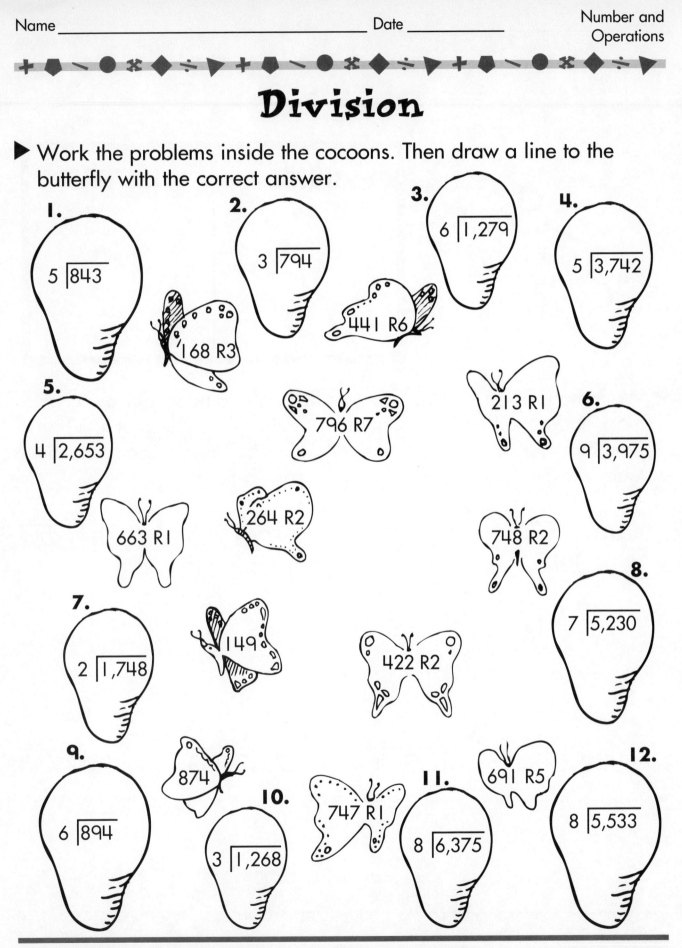

1. $5 \overline{)843}$

2. $3 \overline{)794}$

168 R3

441 R6

3. $6 \overline{)1,279}$

4. $5 \overline{)3,742}$

5. $4 \overline{)2,653}$

796 R7

213 R1

6. $9 \overline{)3,975}$

663 R1

264 R2

748 R2

7. $2 \overline{)1,748}$

149

422 R2

8. $7 \overline{)5,230}$

9. $6 \overline{)894}$

874

10. $3 \overline{)1,268}$

747 R1

11. $8 \overline{)6,375}$

691 R5

12. $8 \overline{)5,533}$

Division

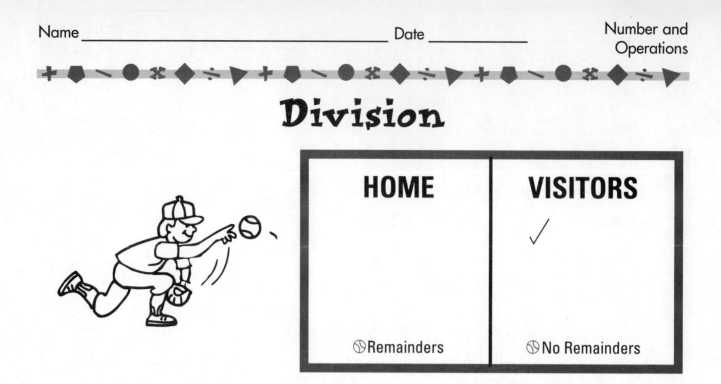

	HOME	VISITORS
		✓
	Remainders	No Remainders

▶ Work the problems. If the problem has a remainder, place a check mark under the Home team on the scoreboard. If the problem has no remainder, place a check mark under the Visitor team. Which team wins?

1.
$$\begin{array}{r} 39 \\ 49\overline{)1,911} \\ 147 \\ \hline 441 \\ 441 \\ \hline 0 \end{array}$$

2. $21\overline{)657}$

3. $52\overline{)3,796}$

4. $64\overline{)2,752}$

5. $42\overline{)967}$

6. $32\overline{)999}$

7. $73\overline{)3,069}$

8. $43\overline{)2,763}$

Division Problem Solving

► The 5 members of the Porter family decided to visit Denali National Park for their summer vacation. Read each problem. Write the answer on the line and the problem you used to find it.

1. The Porter family will eat 30 meals while they are in the park. To be fair, each of the 5 family members chooses the place to eat an equal number of times. How many times will each person choose? _____

2. Mr. Porter bought a set of 24 postcards for everyone in the family to share. How many will each person get to send to friends back home, and how many will be left to put in the scrapbook? _____

3. The family went to a ranger talk. They learned that there had been one large moose herd with 96 moose in it. The herd had been divided evenly into 6 smaller herds. How many moose were in each herd? _____

4. A maximum of 72 tourists can go on the Horseshoe Lake walk. If the walk is full and there are 8 rangers leading groups, how many tourists will be in each group? _____

5. The family shared a sightseeing bus with other tourists. There were 36 seats. The bus had 9 full rows of seats. How many seats were in each row? _____

Name _____ Date _____

Mixed Operations

▶ Solve each line to find the treasure.

1.

2.

3.

4.

▶ Add the total treasure.

Published by Instructional Fair. Copyright protected.   0-7424-1721-2 Math

Name_____ Date _____

Mixed Operations

▶ Decide which operation (+, −, x, ÷) solves the square.
Work the squares.

	6	2	4	7	1
5	30				
8		16			
3				21	
9			36		

	82	53	41	54	62
16	66				46
21	61				
18			23		
32					30

	23	15	31	89	58
19	42				
57			88		
63					121
45				136	

	6	3	8	4	1
4	24				
9				36	
5					5
7		21			

▶ Which sign was not used? _____

Published by Instructional Fair. Copyright protected.
43
0-7424-1721-2 Math

Averaging

Average—The result of
dividing the sum of addends
by the number of addends.

$$\begin{array}{r} 62 \\ 79 \\ + \ 87 \\ \hline 228 \end{array}$$

$$3\overline{)228}^{\,76}$$

▶ Add the numbers. Then divide by the number of addends. Match
the problem with the answer.

1. 80 + 100 + 90 + 95 + 100	•	A. 53
2. 52 + 56 + 51	•	B. 190
3. 85 + 80 + 95 + 95 + 100	•	C. 410
4. 782 + 276 + 172	•	D. 91
5. 125 + 248 + 214 + 173	•	E. 93
6. 81 + 82 + 91 + 78	•	F. 55
7. 40 + 60 + 75 + 45	•	G. 83
8. 278 + 246	•	H. 33
9. 75 + 100 + 100 + 70 + 100	•	I. 3
10. 0 + 0 + 0 + 0 + 15	•	J. 262
11. 21 + 34 + 44	•	K. 89
12. 437 + 509 + 864 + 274	•	L. 94
13. 80 + 80 + 100 + 95 + 95	•	M. 8
14. 4 + 6 + 7 + 12 + 11	•	N. 90
15. 75 + 100 + 100 + 100 + 95	•	O. 521

Averaging

▶ Find the average for the numbers given. Find the letter with the correct answer and add it to the riddle.

1. 25 16 18 33	2. 98 75 82 92 83	3. 30 80 40 24 38 16	4. 16 20 15	5. 29 60 52	6. 57 18 32 42 57 88
7. 9 11 9 15	8. 31 29 41 39	9. 81 57 63	10. 34 43 28 51	11. 50 81 96 77	12. 5 12 8 7

A	23
!	8
C	83
I	76
B	9
E	38
P	67
R	17
M	48
O	31
T	11
Z	40

W	47
L	35
S	5
F	39
U	24
N	88
G	86
K	69
H	49
Q	79
D	13
J	14

What is purple and goes thump, thump?

___   ___ ___ ___ ___ ___
23   86 17 23 67 38

___ ___ ___ ___   ___
47 76 11 49   23

___ ___ ___ ___   ___ ___ ___ ___ ___
39 35 23 11   11 76 17 38 8

Fractions

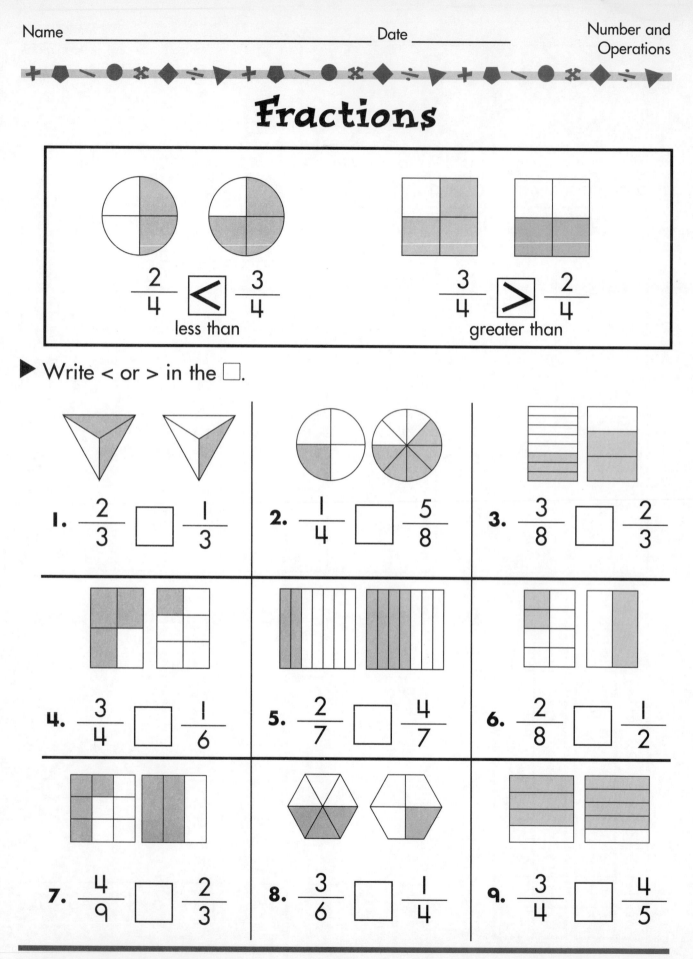

$\dfrac{2}{4}$ < $\dfrac{3}{4}$
less than

$\dfrac{3}{4}$ > $\dfrac{2}{4}$
greater than

▶ Write < or > in the ☐.

1. $\dfrac{2}{3}$ ☐ $\dfrac{1}{3}$

2. $\dfrac{1}{4}$ ☐ $\dfrac{5}{8}$

3. $\dfrac{3}{8}$ ☐ $\dfrac{2}{3}$

4. $\dfrac{3}{4}$ ☐ $\dfrac{1}{6}$

5. $\dfrac{2}{7}$ ☐ $\dfrac{4}{7}$

6. $\dfrac{2}{8}$ ☐ $\dfrac{1}{2}$

7. $\dfrac{4}{9}$ ☐ $\dfrac{2}{3}$

8. $\dfrac{3}{6}$ ☐ $\dfrac{1}{4}$

9. $\dfrac{3}{4}$ ☐ $\dfrac{4}{5}$

Fractions

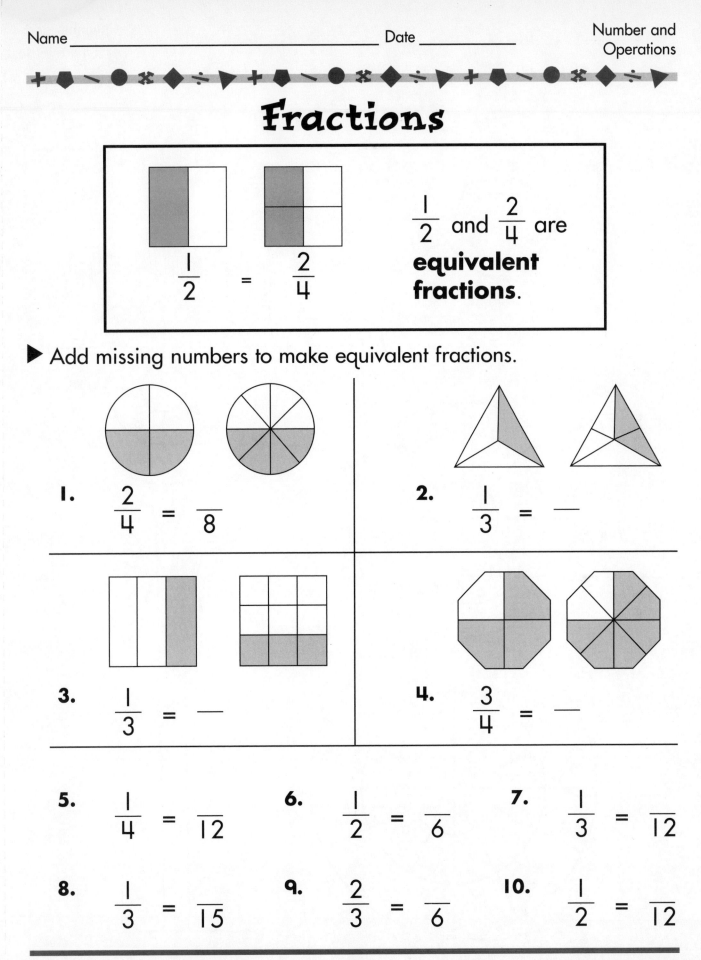

$\dfrac{1}{2}$ and $\dfrac{2}{4}$ are **equivalent fractions**.

$\dfrac{1}{2}$ = $\dfrac{2}{4}$

▶ Add missing numbers to make equivalent fractions.

1. $\dfrac{2}{4} = \dfrac{}{8}$

2. $\dfrac{1}{3} = \dfrac{}{}$

3. $\dfrac{1}{3} = \dfrac{}{}$

4. $\dfrac{3}{4} = \dfrac{}{}$

5. $\dfrac{1}{4} = \dfrac{}{12}$

6. $\dfrac{1}{2} = \dfrac{}{6}$

7. $\dfrac{1}{3} = \dfrac{}{12}$

8. $\dfrac{1}{3} = \dfrac{}{15}$

9. $\dfrac{2}{3} = \dfrac{}{6}$

10. $\dfrac{1}{2} = \dfrac{}{12}$

Fractions

▶ Add center fraction with fraction in next row to fill in outer row.

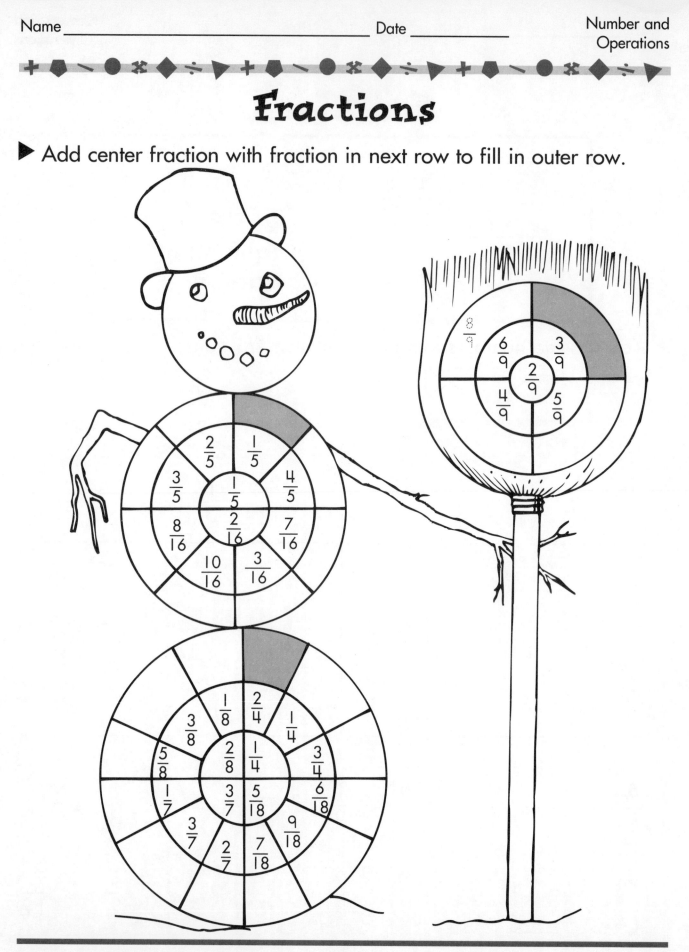

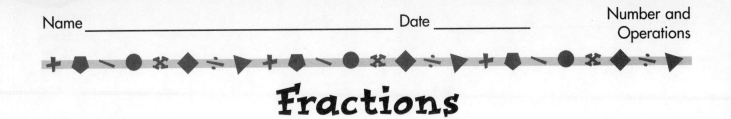

Fractions

▶ Subtract the fractions. Cross out the letter in the decoder that matches your answer. The remaining letters give the answer to the riddle.

1. $\dfrac{7}{8}$
   $-\dfrac{2}{8}$

2. $\dfrac{3}{4}$
   $-\dfrac{1}{4}$

3. $\dfrac{6}{7}$
   $-\dfrac{3}{7}$

4. $\dfrac{5}{6}$
   $-\dfrac{2}{6}$

5. $\dfrac{11}{12}$
   $-\dfrac{5}{12}$

6. $\dfrac{14}{16}$
   $-\dfrac{7}{16}$

7. $\dfrac{4}{5}$
   $-\dfrac{1}{5}$

8. $\dfrac{9}{10}$
   $-\dfrac{5}{10}$

▶ What kind of beans will not grow in a garden?

___ ___ ___ ___ ___ **beans**.

A $\frac{3}{7}$	M $\frac{4}{10}$	J $\frac{10}{20}$	E $\frac{4}{6}$	O $\frac{6}{12}$
C $\frac{3}{5}$	V $\frac{2}{4}$	A $\frac{7}{16}$	D $\frac{5}{8}$	L $\frac{7}{10}$
I $\frac{3}{6}$	L $\frac{8}{16}$	Y $\frac{1}{4}$		

Published by Instructional Fair. Copyright protected.

0-7424-1721-2 Math

Fractions

▶ Reduce to lowest terms. Shade each part that is equivalent to $\frac{1}{2}$ or $\frac{2}{3}$. How do you spell mousetrap with just 4 letters?

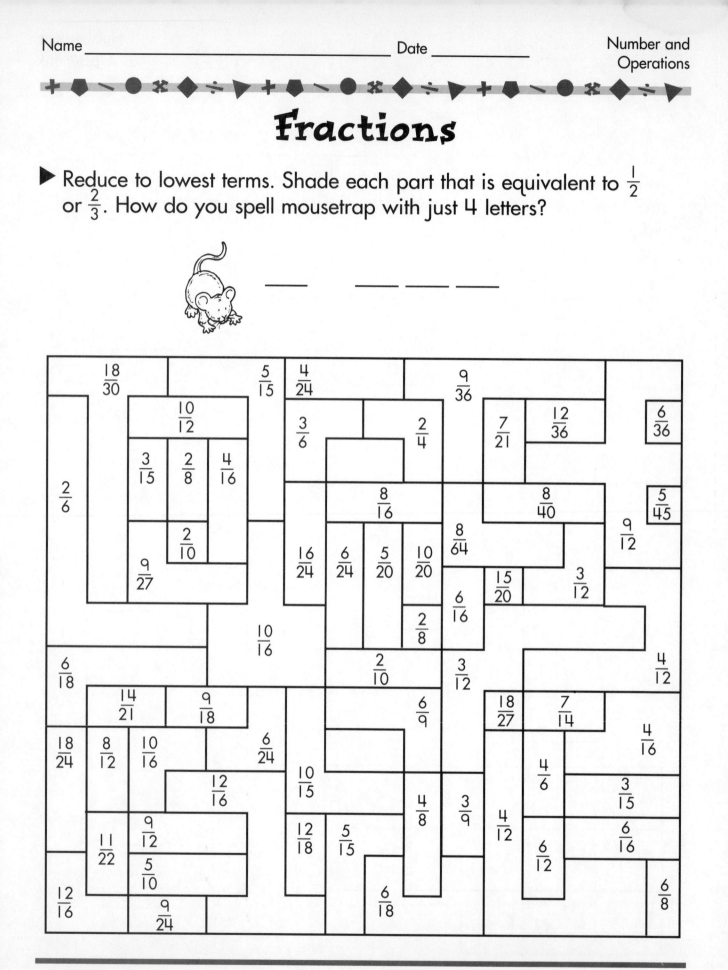

Decimals

Decimal Point—A dot placed between the ones
place and the tenths place.

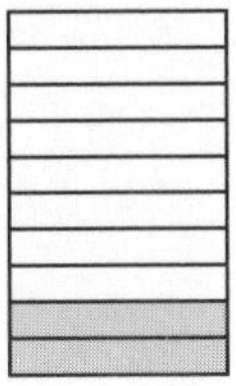

.2 is read as
two tenths.

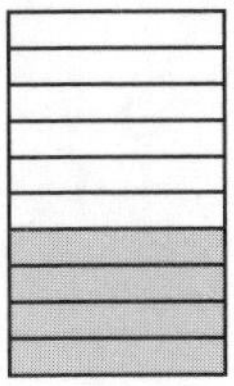

.4 is read as
four tenths.

▶ Express the shaded parts as a decimal.

1. 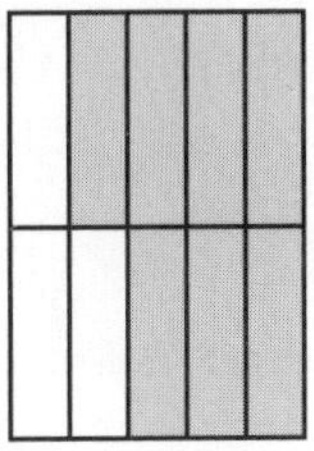
.7

2.
_____

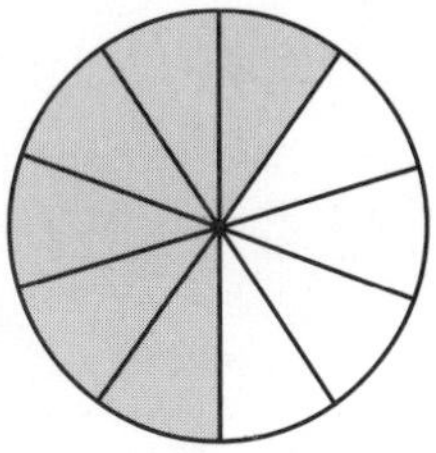

3.
_____

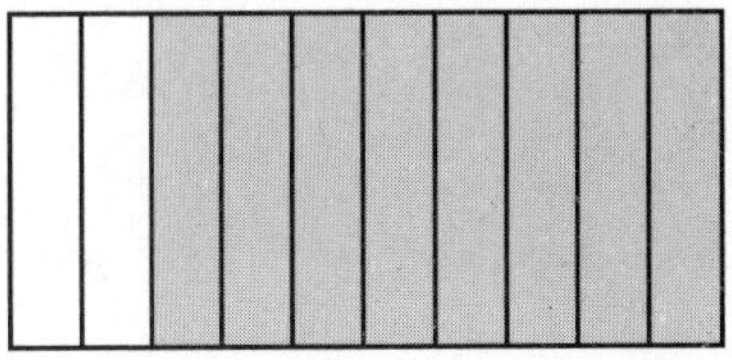

4.
_____

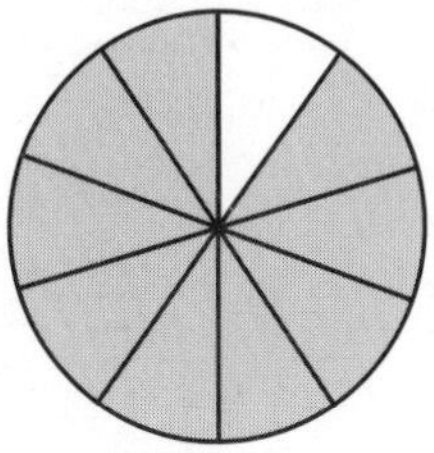

5.
_____

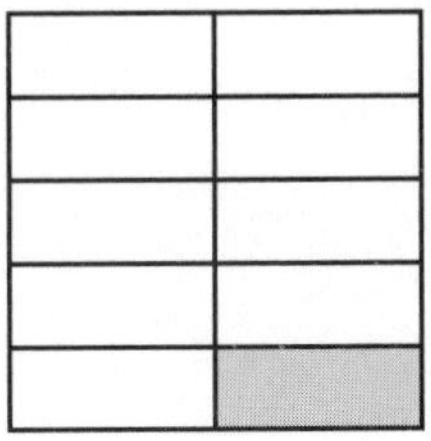

6.
_____

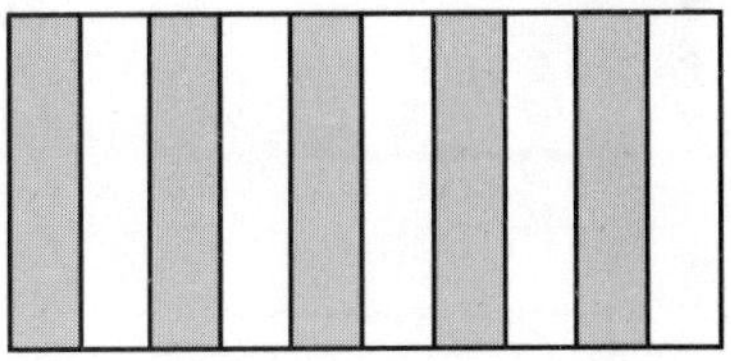

▶ Color parts to match decimals.

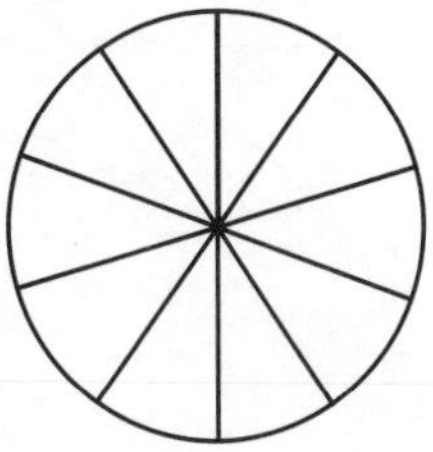

.4

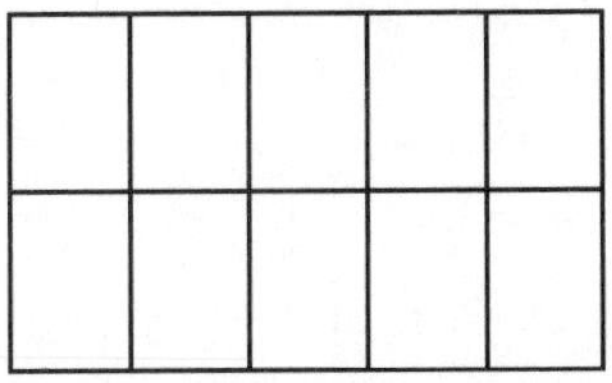

.3

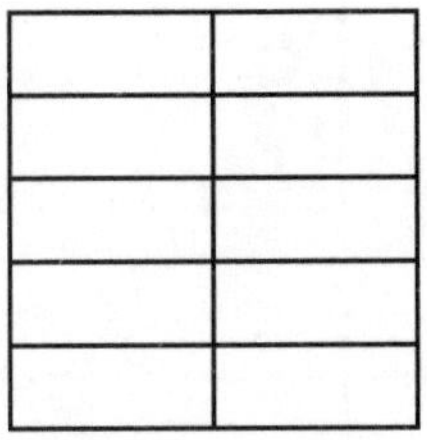

.2

Decimals

▶ When you add or subtract decimals, remember to include the decimal in your answer.

1.
$$\begin{array}{r} 4.2 \\ +\ 5.2 \\ \hline \end{array}$$

2.
$$\begin{array}{r} 6.4 \\ +\ 1.4 \\ \hline \end{array}$$

3.
$$\begin{array}{r} 3.1 \\ +\ 7.8 \\ \hline \end{array}$$

4.
$$\begin{array}{r} 4.7 \\ +\ 3.2 \\ \hline \end{array}$$

5.
$$\begin{array}{r} 4.9 \\ +\ 2.0 \\ \hline \end{array}$$

6.
$$\begin{array}{r} 5.9 \\ -\ 3.2 \\ \hline \end{array}$$

7.
$$\begin{array}{r} 6.7 \\ -\ 5.6 \\ \hline \end{array}$$

8.
$$\begin{array}{r} 7.8 \\ -\ 2.5 \\ \hline \end{array}$$

9.
$$\begin{array}{r} 5.8 \\ -\ 3.3 \\ \hline \end{array}$$

10.
$$\begin{array}{r} 3.9 \\ -\ 1.5 \\ \hline \end{array}$$

11.
$$\begin{array}{r} .23 \\ +\ .25 \\ \hline \end{array}$$

12.
$$\begin{array}{r} .43 \\ +\ .16 \\ \hline \end{array}$$

13.
$$\begin{array}{r} .26 \\ +\ .42 \\ \hline \end{array}$$

14.
$$\begin{array}{r} .64 \\ +\ .15 \\ \hline \end{array}$$

15.
$$\begin{array}{r} .68 \\ +\ .31 \\ \hline \end{array}$$

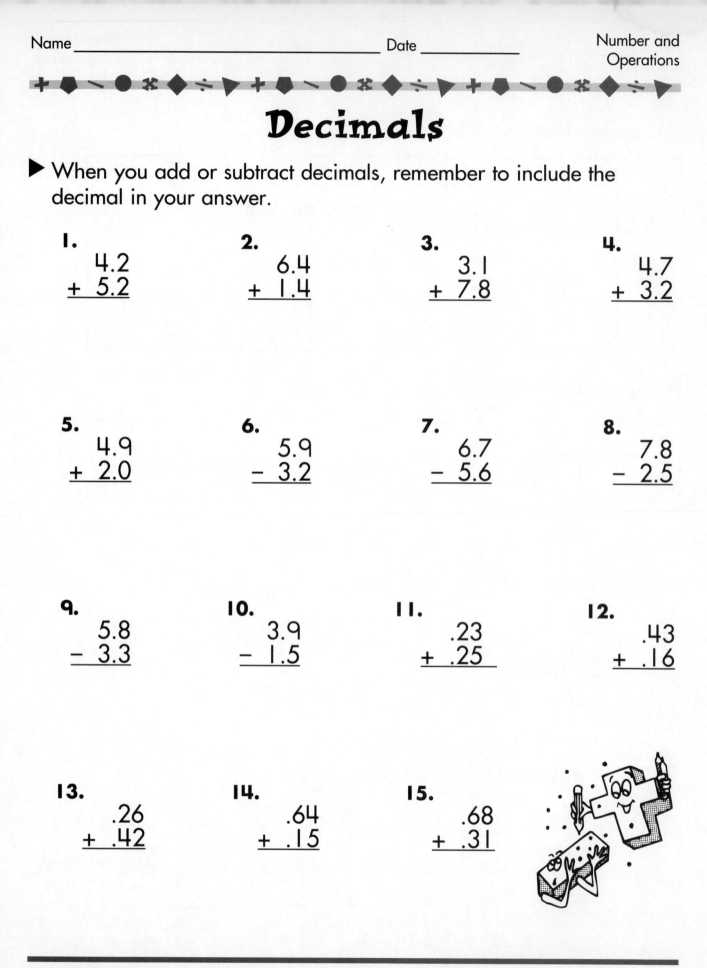

Money

▶ Read the directions. Give the total amount of spending money.

1. Melissa has 6 coins. One-half $\left(\frac{1}{2}\right)$ are dimes, two-sixths $\left(\frac{2}{6}\right)$ are pennies, and the rest are nickels. How much does Melissa have?

_____

2. Jamal has 9 coins. One-third $\left(\frac{1}{3}\right)$ are half-dollars, four-ninths $\left(\frac{4}{9}\right)$ are nickels, and the rest are dimes. How much does Jamal have?

_____

3. Samantha has 4 coins. One-fourth $\left(\frac{1}{4}\right)$ are quarters, one-half $\left(\frac{1}{2}\right)$ are pennies, and the rest are dimes. How much does Samantha have?

_____

4. Mariana has 8 coins. One-half $\left(\frac{1}{2}\right)$ are pennies, one-fourth $\left(\frac{1}{4}\right)$ are nickels, and the rest are half-dollars. How much does Mariana have?

_____

5. Brian has 12 coins. One-half $\left(\frac{1}{2}\right)$ are quarters, one-third $\left(\frac{1}{3}\right)$ are dimes, and the rest are pennies. How much does Brian have? _____

6. Michael has 10 coins. Three-tenths $\left(\frac{3}{10}\right)$ are dimes, one-fifth $\left(\frac{1}{5}\right)$ are quarters, and the rest are half-dollars. How much does Michael have?

_____

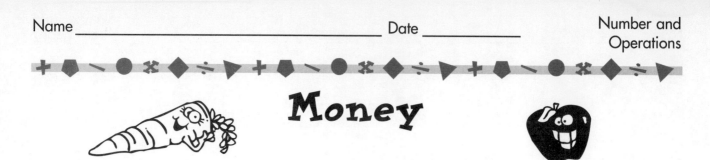

Money

▶ Kamarah and her class are learning about fruits and vegetables. They went to the grocery store to compare prices. Help Kamarah complete the total cost and change back for all of the produce on the class list.

Produce	Price per Pound	Pounds Bought	Total Cost	Paid With	Change Back
apples	82¢	5		$5.00	
blueberries	67¢	3		$2.25	
broccoli	52¢	7		$5.00	
cantaloupe	83¢	8		$10.00	
carrots	27¢	3		$1.00	
cucumbers	36¢	6		$3.00	
green beans	48¢	2		$1.00	
kiwi	30¢	11		$5.00	
peaches	98¢	9		$10.00	
pears	78¢	4		$5.00	
strawberries	93¢	5		$5.00	
tomatoes	86¢	7		$10.00	

Shape Patterns

▶ Each problem below contains three sets of shapes. One shape has been left out of each set. Study the pattern, then draw the missing shape inside the dotted oval.

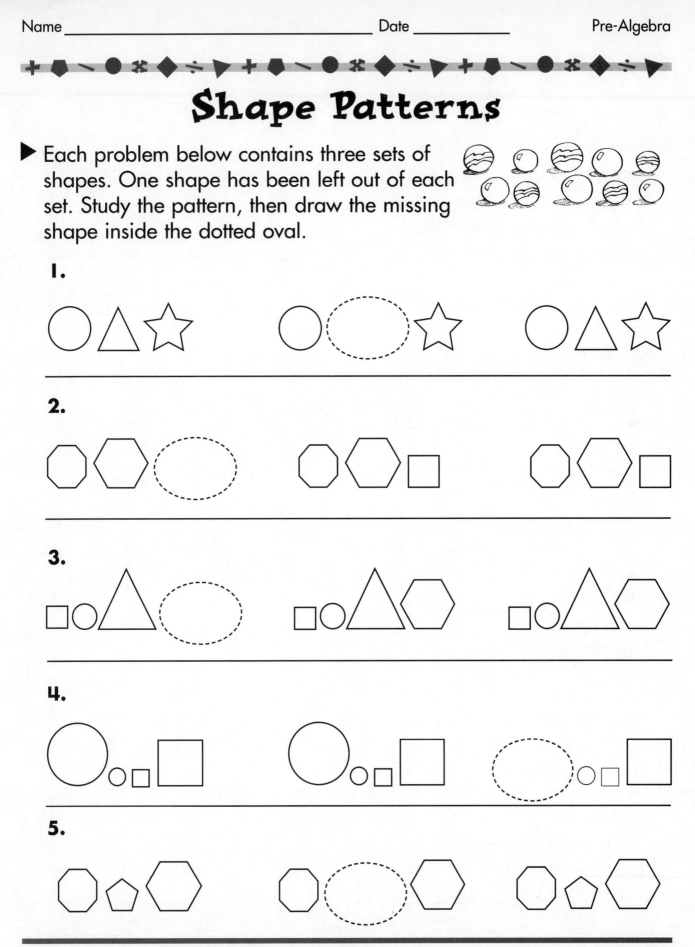

1.

2.

3.

4.

5.

Number Patterns

▶ Find the pattern in each row of numbers. Continue the pattern to fill in the blanks. Then match the pattern to the correct rule.

Pattern	**Rule**
1, 3, 5, ___, ___, 11, 13	– 11
70, ___, 50, ___, ___, 20, 10	+ 12
1, 8, 15, 22, ___, ___, ___	+ 8
36, 33, 30, ___, ___, ___, ___	– 9
115, 100, 85, ___, ___, ___, ___	+ 2
64, 55, 46, ___, ___, ___, ___	– 10
17, 25, 33, ___, ___, ___, ___	– 3
96, ___, 84, 78, ___, ___, ___	– 15
88, ___, 66, ___, 44, ___, ___	– 6
12, 24, 36, ___, ___, ___, ___	+ 7

Name _____ Date _____ Pre-Algebra

Number Patterns

► Some numbers are missing from the chart below. Look for patterns and then fill in the chart before you answer the questions.

Hint: Which operation is this table based on (+, −, x, ÷)?

1		3			6			9	10
2	4			10			16		20
3			12			21			30
4		12		24				36	40
5	10			25		40			50
6			24			42			60
7		21			42			63	70
8	16			40			64		80
9			36			63			90
10		30			60				100

1. Circle all the odd numbers. How many squares have circles? _____

2. Put an X over the following number patterns when you find them in the grid:
   20, 27, 32, 35, 36, 35, 32, 27, 20
   5, 8, 9, 8, 5
   8, 14, 18, 20, 20, 18, 14, 8
   50, 54, 56, 56, 54, 50

3. How many squares have both a circle and an X? _____

Missing Values

▶ Fill in the box with the operation symbol needed to make the number sentence true.

Example: 3 $\boxed{+}$ 2 = 5

1. 7 ☐ 3 = 10

2. 15 ☐ 5 = 20

3. 13 ☐ 7 = 6

4. 3 ☐ 2 = 6

5. 4 ☐ 2 = 8

6. 12 ☐ 6 = 6

7. 23 ☐ 3 = 26

8. 10 ☐ 5 = 2

9. 49 ☐ 19 = 68

10. 21 ☐ 4 = 17

11. 12 ☐ 2 = 24

12. 19 ☐ 3 = 22

13. 17 ☐ 7 = 10

14. 3 ☐ 18 = 21

15. 2 ☐ 5 = 10

16. 7 ☐ 6 = 42

17. 32 ☐ 4 = 28

18. 16 ☐ 4 = 4

19. 5 ☐ 6 = 11

20. 31 ☐ 1 = 30

Missing Values

▶ Fill in the missing number to show equal values.

Example: $2 + 10 = \boxed{4} + 8$

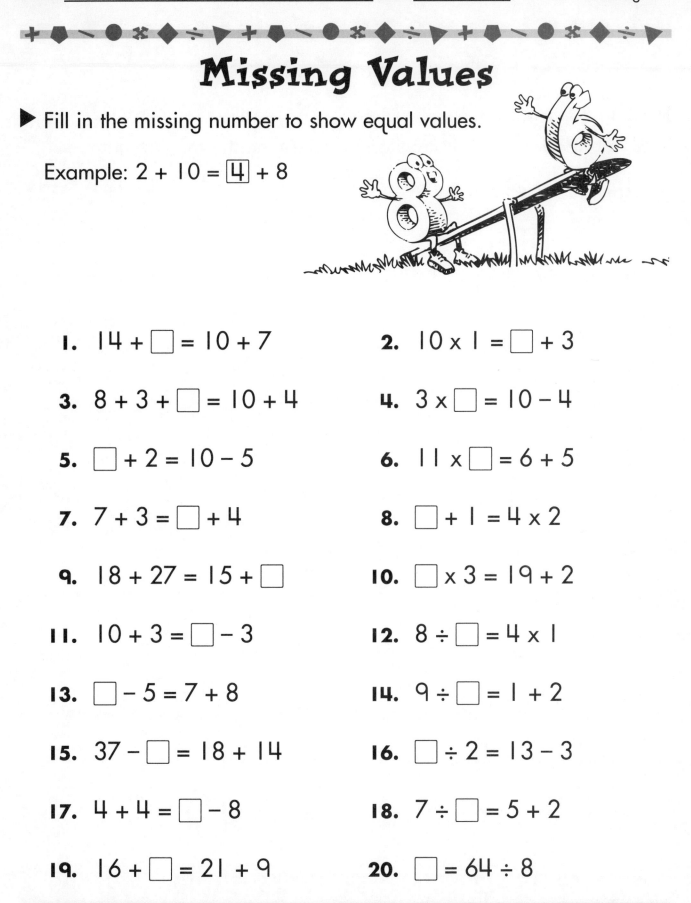

1. $14 + \square = 10 + 7$

2. $10 \times 1 = \square + 3$

3. $8 + 3 + \square = 10 + 4$

4. $3 \times \square = 10 - 4$

5. $\square + 2 = 10 - 5$

6. $11 \times \square = 6 + 5$

7. $7 + 3 = \square + 4$

8. $\square + 1 = 4 \times 2$

9. $18 + 27 = 15 + \square$

10. $\square \times 3 = 19 + 2$

11. $10 + 3 = \square - 3$

12. $8 \div \square = 4 \times 1$

13. $\square - 5 = 7 + 8$

14. $9 \div \square = 1 + 2$

15. $37 - \square = 18 + 14$

16. $\square \div 2 = 13 - 3$

17. $4 + 4 = \square - 8$

18. $7 \div \square = 5 + 2$

19. $16 + \square = 21 + 9$

20. $\square = 64 \div 8$

Number Letters

► Each problem has a letter in place of a number. Use what you know about addition and subtraction to determine the missing number.

1. $3 + m = 29$

m = _____

2. $17 + 7 = a + 8$

a = _____

3. $33 + 17 = s - 8$

s = _____

4. $55 - 17 = t$

t = _____

5. $u + 3 = 18 + 16$

u = _____

6. $23 + 15 = 19 + o$

o = _____

7. $b + 23 = 43$

b = _____

8. $f = 27 + 46$

f = _____

9. $75 - e = 30 + 5$

e = _____

10. $2 + d = 49 + 5$

d = _____

11. $24 = r + 1$

r = _____

12. $l = 31 - 9$

l = _____

13. $47 = n + 5$

n = _____

14. $7 + g = 14 + 11$

g = _____

15. $c = 21 - 4$

c = _____

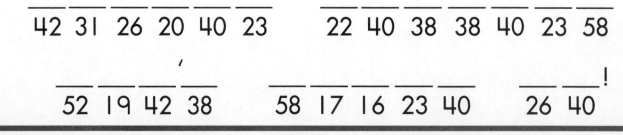

► Use the answers from the problems above to fill in the letters below and reveal a message.

___ ___ ___ ___ ___ ___   ___ ___ ___ ___ ___ ___ ___
42 31 26 20 40 23   22 40 38 38 40 23 58

,

___ ___ ___ ___   ___ ___ ___ ___ ___   ___ ___!
52 19 42 38   58 17 16 23 40   26 40

Number Pyramids

▶ Add adjacent numbers together. Write their sum in the block above them. Continue adding until you reach the top block.

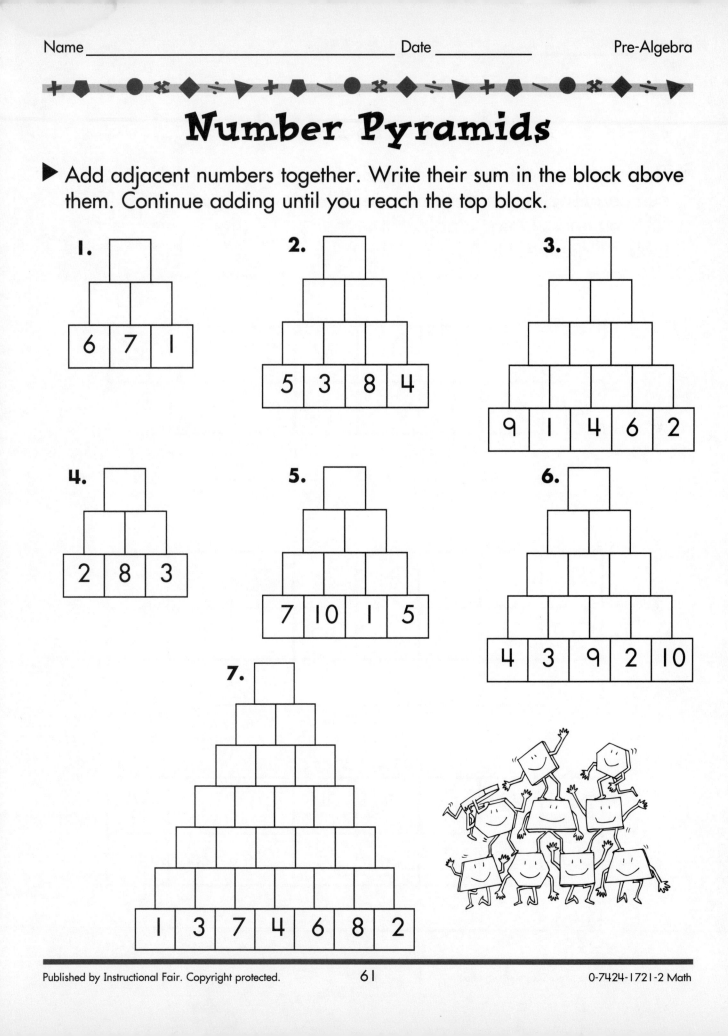

1.

| 6 | 7 | 1 |

2.

| 5 | 3 | 8 | 4 |

3.

| 9 | 1 | 4 | 6 | 2 |

4.

| 2 | 8 | 3 |

5.

| 7 | 10 | 1 | 5 |

6.

| 4 | 3 | 9 | 2 | 10 |

7.

| 1 | 3 | 7 | 4 | 6 | 8 | 2 |

Find the Rule

▶ The function machine uses rules to change numbers. Look for a pattern in the IN and OUT numbers in each table. Fill in the table. Write the rule.

IN	78	15	41	22	37		55
OUT	65	2	28			3	

Rule: _____

IN	2	9	81	76	37		
OUT	11	18		85		34	51

Rule: _____

IN	82	16	70	34	44		60
OUT	41	8			22	25	

Rule: _____

Name_____ Date _____ Pre-Algebra

Pre-Algebra Problem Solving

▶ The third, fourth, and fifth graders from Thomas Jefferson Elementary school had an ice cream party. The students voted for chocolate, strawberry, or vanilla ice cream. How many votes did each kind of ice cream receive in each grade? What is the total number of votes for each flavor for all three grades?

KEY
C = Chocolate
S = Strawberry
V = Vanilla

Third Grade
14 votes for chocolate, $\frac{1}{2}$ as many votes for strawberry as for chocolate, 25 votes in all.

C = _____ S = _____
V = _____

Total Votes

C = _____

S = _____

V = _____

Fourth Grade
No votes for vanilla, an equal number of votes for chocolate and strawberry, 32 votes in all.

C = _____ S = _____
V = _____

Fifth Grade
8 votes for chocolate, twice as many votes for strawberry, 28 votes in all.

C = _____ S = _____
V = _____

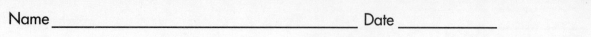

What's a Polygon?

► Two-dimensional shapes can be grouped into categories like open or closed, polygon or non-polygon. See if you can guess the definition of a polygon by looking at the examples below. Hint: Are polygons open or closed figures? What kind of sides do polygons have?

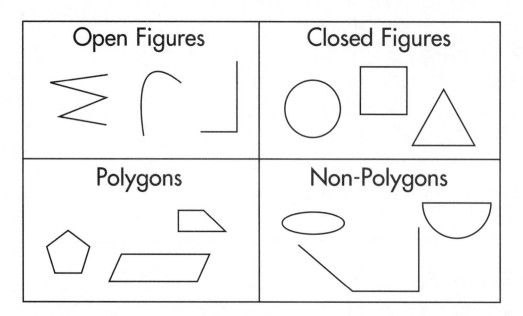

1. Based on the examples above, list the characteristics that all polygons have in common.

   _____

2. What characteristics would let you know the shape is not a polygon?

   _____

3. A polygon is a closed two-dimensional figure that has straight sides. How close was your definition?

   _____

Types of Triangles

Right Triangle—One of the angles measures 90 degrees (an L-shaped angle)

Acute Triangles—All angles in the triangle measure less than 90 degrees

Obtuse Triangles—One of the angles measures more than 90 degrees

Isosceles Triangles—Two of the sides are equal

Equilateral Triangle—All three sides are equal

Scalene Triangle—No sides are equal

▶ Follow the instructions for each type of triangle. Remember, triangles can be more than one type.

- Color all the **right** triangles blue.
- Color all the **acute** triangles red.
- Color all the **obtuse** triangles green.
- Circle all the **isosceles** triangles.
- Put a box around all the **equilateral** triangles.
- Put a line beneath all the **scalene** triangles.

Quadrilaterals

▶ A **quadrilateral** is any figure with 4 sides and 4 angles. Some quadrilaterals have special names.

Trapezoid—a quadrilateral with 1 set of parallel sides
Parallelogram—a quadrilateral with 2 sets of parallel sides
Rectangle—a quadrilateral with 4 right angles and

opposite sides of equal length
Square—a quadrilateral with 4 right angles and 4 equal sides
Rhombus—a quadrilateral with 4 equal sides and 2 pairs of parallel sides

▶ Classify the following shapes as **quadrilateral, trapezoid, parallelogram, rectangle, square,** or **rhombus.**

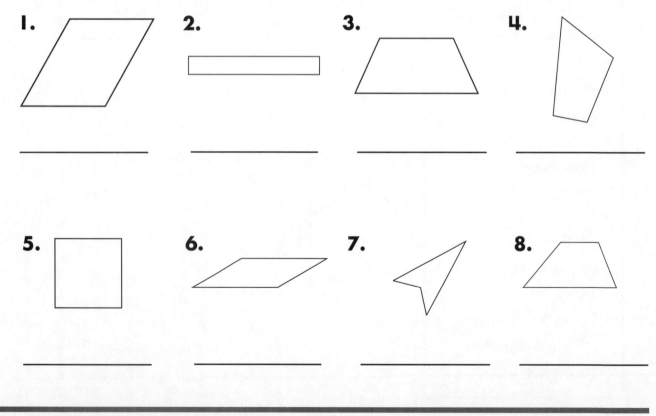

1. _____

2. _____

3. _____

4. _____

5. _____

6. _____

7. _____

8. _____

0-7424-1721-2 Math

Types of Polygons

The word **polygon** means "many sides." Polygons are grouped into different categories based on their number of sides and angles, as shown in the chart. A shape with any curved sides is not a polygon.	Polygon Name	Number of Sides and Angles
	a. Triangle	3
	b. Quadrilateral	4
	c. Pentagon	5
	d. Hexagon	6
	e. Heptagon	7
	f. Octagon	8
	g. Not a polygon	

▶ Put the letter of the polygon name that matches each shape in the blank next to the shape. Or, if the shape is not a polygon, put the letter *g* in the blank. The polygon names may be used more than once.

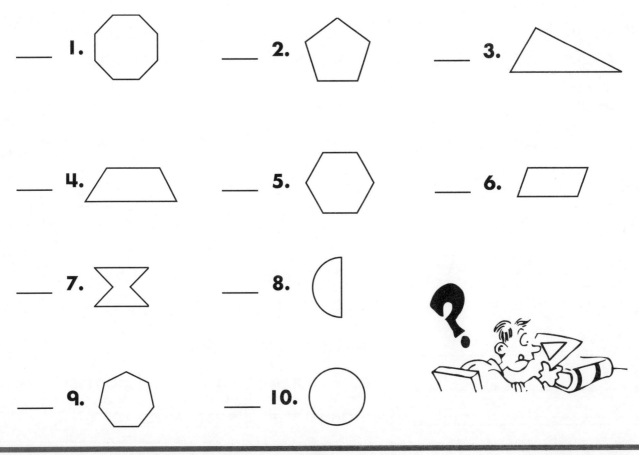

___ 1.   ___ 2.   ___ 3.

___ 4.   ___ 5.   ___ 6.

___ 7.   ___ 8.

___ 9.   ___ 10.

Identifying Polygons

▶ Identify 8 different polygons in the drawing below. Be as specific as possible when naming polygons (e.g., "scalene triangle" rather than simply "triangle").

▶ Fill in the blanks with the names of polygons you found in the picture above. Match each polygon to its correct definition.

_____ 1. polygon with 8 sides

_____ 2. quadrilateral with 4 right angles and 4 equal sides

_____ 3. quadrilateral with 1 set of parallel sides

_____ 4. triangle with 3 equal sides

_____ 5. quadrilateral with 4 right angles and opposite sides of equal length

_____ 6. polygon with 5 sides

_____ 7. quadrilateral with 2 sets of parallel lines

_____ 8. triangle with 2 equal sides

Dimensions

▶ Match each three-dimensional shape with a corresponding two-dimensional shape by drawing a line. Some shapes will have more than one line.

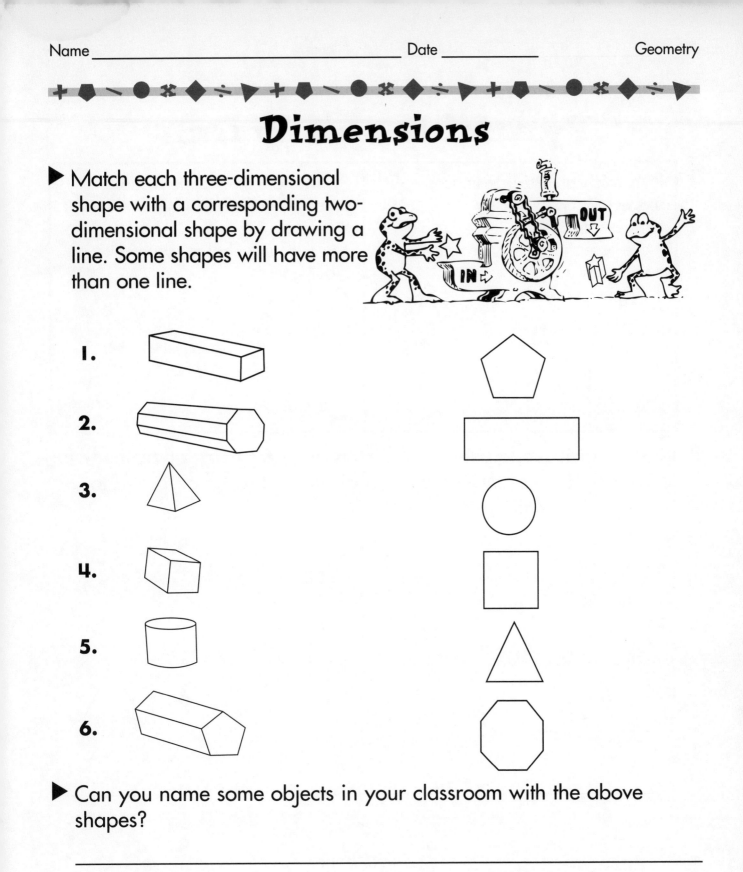

1.

2.

3.

4.

5.

6.

▶ Can you name some objects in your classroom with the above shapes?

_____

_____

_____

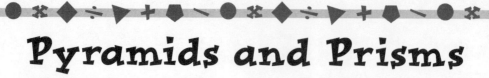

Pyramids and Prisms

Pyramids are three-dimensional shapes with the following characteristics:
- one base shaped like a polygon
- triangular faces
- a point on one end

triangular faces

base

base

Prisms are three-dimensional shapes with the following characteristics:
- two identical bases shaped like polygons
- rectangular faces

base

base

rectangular faces

base

base

▶ Next to each shape below, write **prism**, **pyramid**, or **neither** to show what type of three-dimensional object it is. Be prepared to explain your choices.

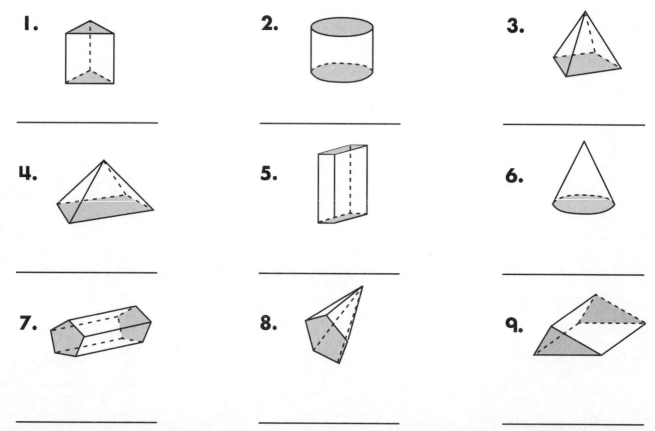

1.

_____

2.

_____

3.

_____

4.

_____

5.

_____

6.

_____

7.

_____

8.

_____

9.

_____

Cones, Cylinders, and Spheres

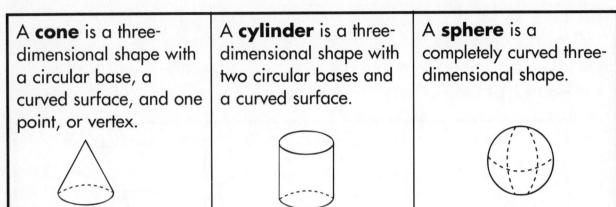

A **cone** is a three-dimensional shape with a circular base, a curved surface, and one point, or vertex.

A **cylinder** is a three-dimensional shape with two circular bases and a curved surface.

A **sphere** is a completely curved three-dimensional shape.

▶ Many everyday objects contain these shapes. For each object shown below, write **cone**, **cylinder**, **sphere**, or **none of these**.

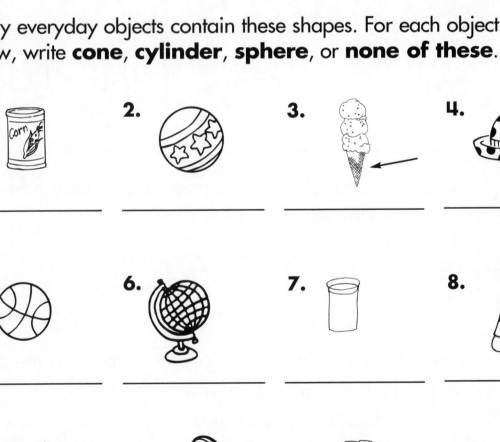

1. _____

2. _____

3. _____

4. _____

5. _____

6. _____

7. _____

8. _____

9. _____

10. _____

11. _____

12. _____

Classifying Prisms

▶ Prisms can be divided into several different categories. The following activities will help you develop criteria for categorizing prisms. Look at each group of prisms. Circle the prism that is different from the others in its group.

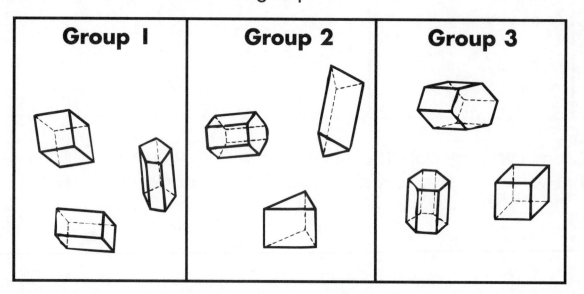

| Group 1 | Group 2 | Group 3 |

1. For each group above, write a sentence describing how the circled shape is different from the others.

Group 1: _____

Group 2: _____

Group 3: _____

2. What characteristic is the same for each prism in the group, but different from the prisms in other groups?
Hint: Compare bases of the prisms.

Group 1: _____

Group 2: _____

Group 3: _____

Congruent or Similar?

Congruent—the same size and shape.	**Similar**—the same shape, but different sizes.

▶ Classify each pair below as **congruent**, **similar**, or **neither**.

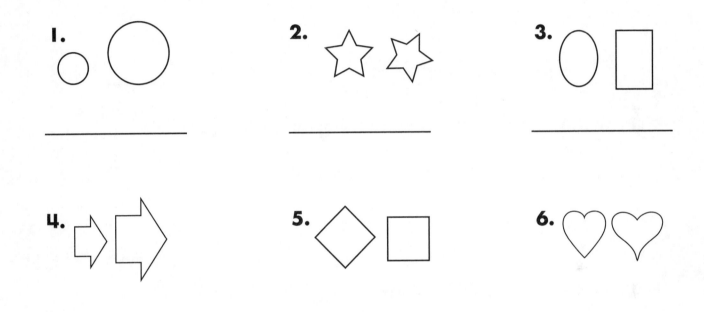

1. _____

2. _____

3. _____

4. _____

5. _____

6. _____

▶ Look at each shape below. Draw a shape that is **similar**.

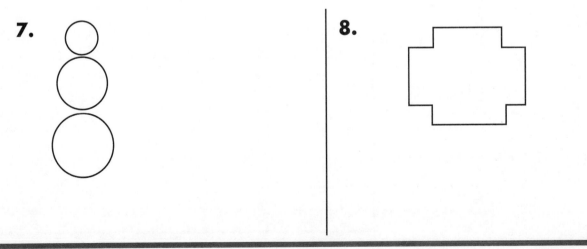

7.

8.

0-7424-1721-2 Math

Symmetry

A figure that can be separated into two matching parts is **symmetric**.

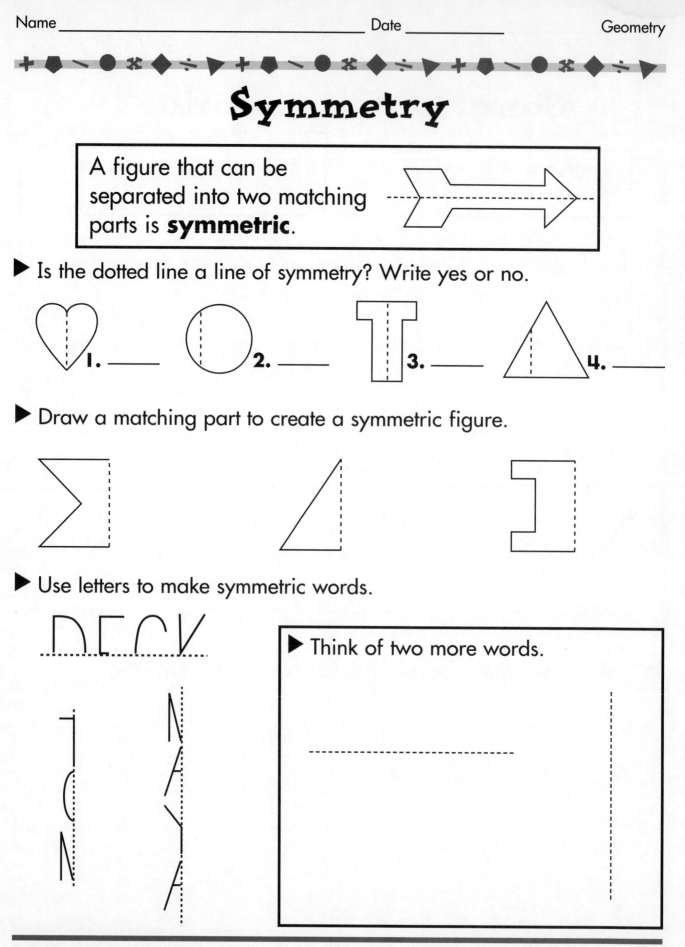

▶ Is the dotted line a line of symmetry? Write yes or no.

1. ___   2. ___   3. ___   4. ___

▶ Draw a matching part to create a symmetric figure.

▶ Use letters to make symmetric words.

DECK

▶ Think of two more words.

Reflection and Rotation

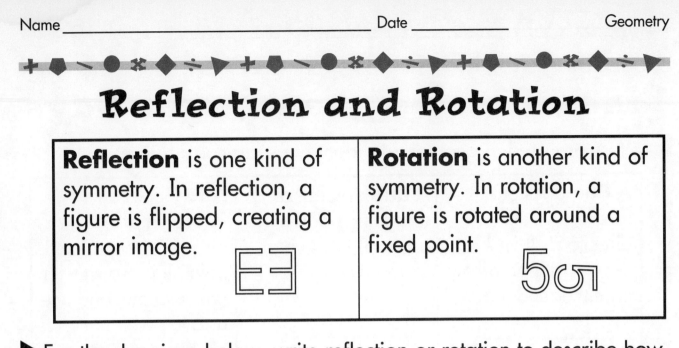

| **Reflection** is one kind of symmetry. In reflection, a figure is flipped, creating a mirror image. | **Rotation** is another kind of symmetry. In rotation, a figure is rotated around a fixed point. |

▶ For the drawings below, write reflection or rotation to describe how the figure was moved.

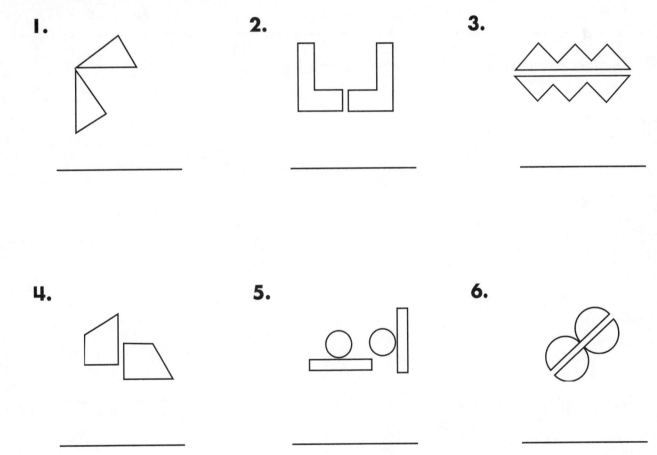

1.

_____

2.

_____

3.

_____

4.

_____

5.

_____

6.

_____

Lines, Line Segments, and Rays

▶ Letters are used in geometry to identify a particular figure.

A **line** goes on forever in both directions. It is drawn with an arrow on either end.	A **line segment** is a specific portion of a line. It has two endpoints.	A **ray** goes on forever in one direction from a fixed point. It is drawn with one endpoint and one arrow.
A • B or $\overleftrightarrow{AB}$	A • B or $\overline{AB}$	A • B or $\overrightarrow{AB}$

▶ Match the name to the correct drawing.

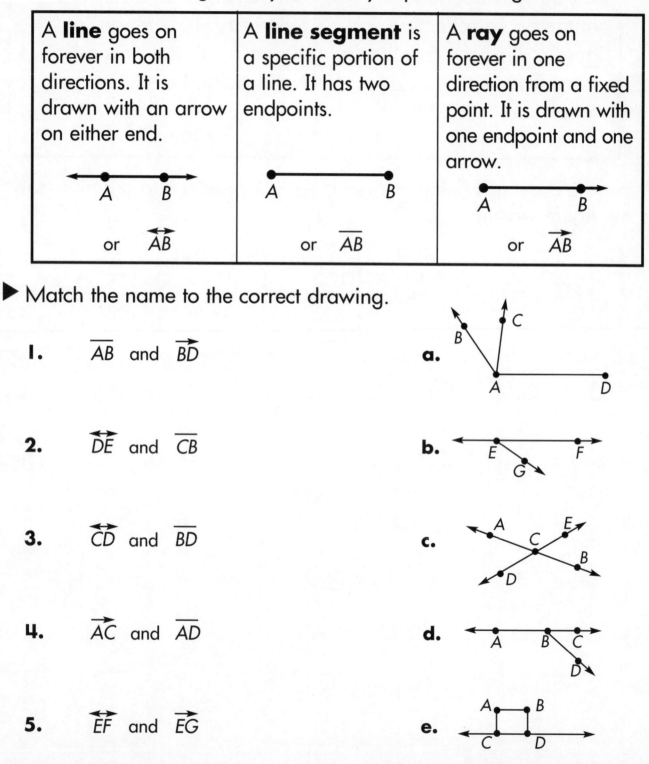

1. $\overline{AB}$ and $\overrightarrow{BD}$

2. $\overleftrightarrow{DE}$ and $\overline{CB}$

3. $\overleftrightarrow{CD}$ and $\overline{BD}$

4. $\overrightarrow{AC}$ and $\overline{AD}$

5. $\overleftrightarrow{EF}$ and $\overrightarrow{EG}$

a.

b.

c.

d.

e.

Parts of a Circle

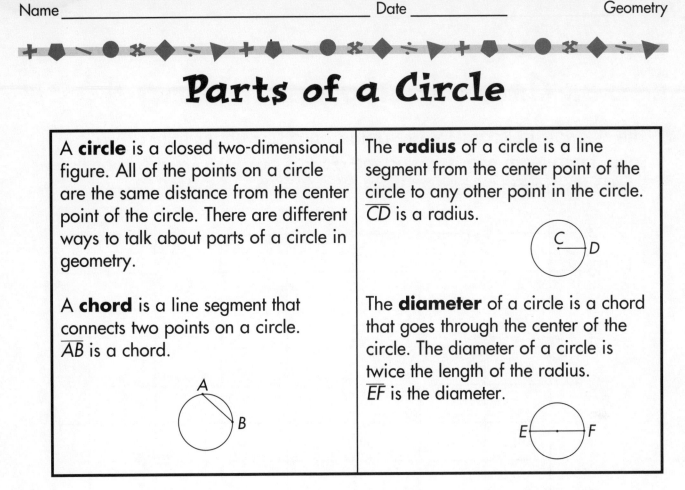

A **circle** is a closed two-dimensional figure. All of the points on a circle are the same distance from the center point of the circle. There are different ways to talk about parts of a circle in geometry.

A **chord** is a line segment that connects two points on a circle. $\overline{AB}$ is a chord.

The **radius** of a circle is a line segment from the center point of the circle to any other point in the circle. $\overline{CD}$ is a radius.

The **diameter** of a circle is a chord that goes through the center of the circle. The diameter of a circle is twice the length of the radius. $\overline{EF}$ is the diameter.

▶ Do the circles below show the same parts? Identify the part(s) of a circle shown for each pair.

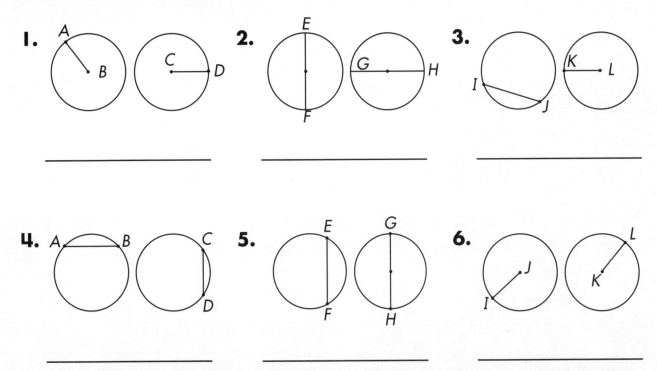

1. _____

2. _____

3. _____

4. _____

5. _____

6. _____

Coordinate Graphing

▶ The students in Room 14 are going on a scavenger hunt at Willow Lake. Each team needs to find the objects below. Give the coordinates where each object can be found.

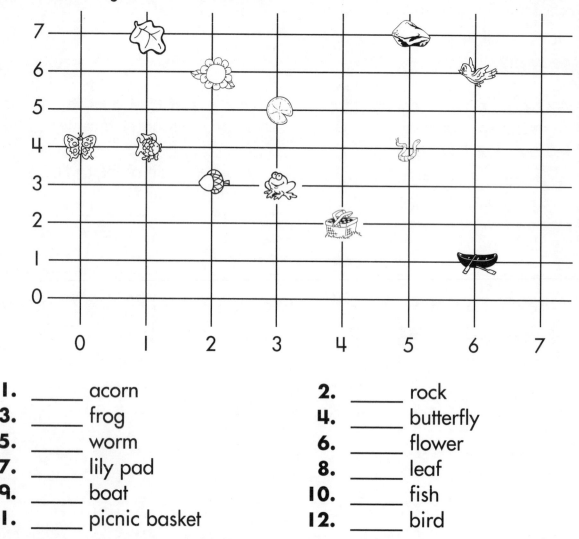

1. _____ acorn		**2.** _____ rock	
3. _____ frog		**4.** _____ butterfly	
5. _____ worm		**6.** _____ flower	
7. _____ lily pad		**8.** _____ leaf	
9. _____ boat		**10.** _____ fish	
11. _____ picnic basket		**12.** _____ bird	

▶ After the scavenger hunt, the students will have a picnic. Help them get ready for the picnic by drawing the given shapes at each coordinate.

apple (5, 2)   juice box (4, 3)
sandwich (3, 1)   carrot (4, 1)

Using a Grid

▶ The letters M, N, and O represent the houses of three friends—
Matt, Nate, and Onan. Each square in the grid represents a square
mile. The heavy black lines on the grid represent roads. Use the grid
to help you answer the questions.

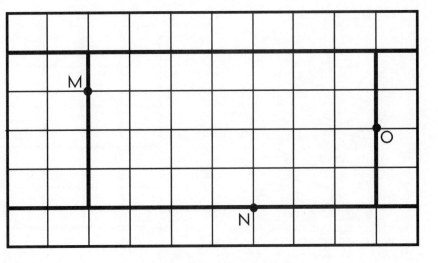

1. Traveling the shortest
distance along the roads,
what is the distance in miles
from Matt's house to Nate's
house? _____

2. Traveling the shortest
distance along the roads,
what is the distance in miles
between Onan's house and
Nate's house?_____

3. Traveling the shortest
distance along the roads,
what is the distance in miles
from Matt's house to
Onan's house? _____

4. Traveling the longest
distance along the roads,
without retracing any part
of the trip, what is the
distance in miles between
Onan's house and Nate's
house? _____

Using a Grid

▶ On the grid below, plot the points that are given at the bottom of this page. Label each point with its corresponding letter. Point L, the library, has been plotted for you at (4, 5). Remember, the first number represents the horizontal axis and the second number represents the vertical axis.

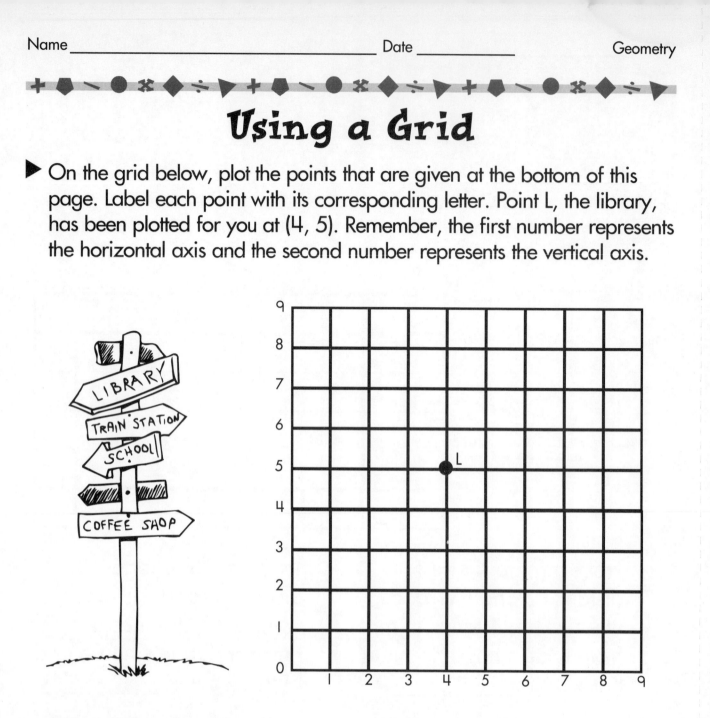

Point C (2, 7) coffee shop   Point P (6, 3) park
Point F (5, 6) fire station   Point S (7, 5) school
Point H (4, 2) hospital   Point T (1, 0) train station

▶ Draw vehicles on the graph and list their coordinates:

A. _____

B. _____

Types of Angles

Right angle—forms a square corner with a measurement of exactly 90°.	**Acute angle**—measures less than 90°.	**Obtuse angle**—measures more than 90°.

▶ Use the definitions to label each angle below.

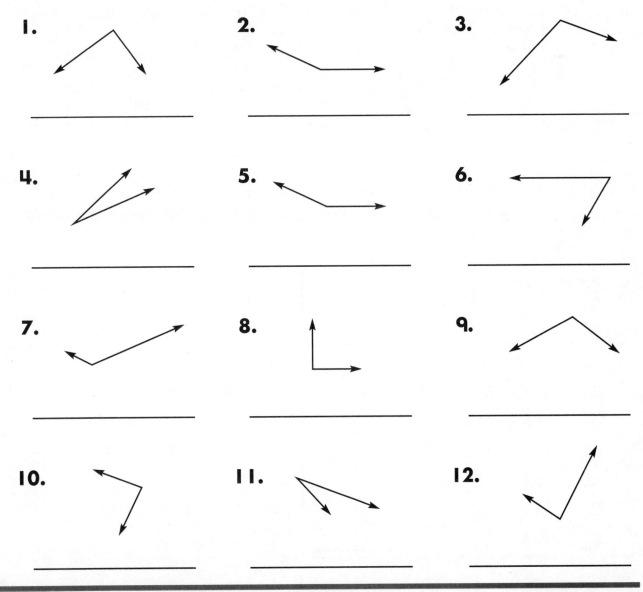

1. _____

2. _____

3. _____

4. _____

5. _____

6. _____

7. _____

8. _____

9. _____

10. _____

11. _____

12. _____

Time Angles

▶ The size of an angle is measured in many ways. One method is to use degrees. The degrees tell you how far you rotated to make the angle. Think of the minute hand on a clock. In one hour, the hand sweeps around in one full circle, ending back where it started. It has made one full turn, which equals 360 degrees, or 360°. This chart shows angles measured by the rotation of a circle, the minutes on a clock, and degrees. Use it to help you with the questions below.

Rotation	Minutes	Degrees
¼ turn	15	90
½ turn	30	180
¾ turn	45	270
full turn	60	360

▶ For each problem, write the degree measure of the angle made when the minute hand on a clock travels from the first time to the second time.

1. 3:15 to 3:30   90 degrees
2. 7:45 to 8:15   _____
3. 4:15 to 5:15   _____
4. 2:00 to 2:45   _____
5. 6:30 to 7:00   _____
6. 11:15 to 11:45   _____
7. 9:30 to 10:00   _____
8. 5:45 to 6:30   _____
9. 4:15 to 5:00   _____
10. 1:30 to 2:00   _____

11. 8:45 to 9:00   _____
12. 4:25 to 4:40   _____
13. 9:30 to 10:30   _____
14. 3:30 to 3:45   _____
15. 4:20 to 4:50   _____
16. 7:03 to 7:48   _____
17. 5:10 to 5:25   _____
18. 2:15 to 2:30   _____
19. 6:04 to 6:49   _____
20. 7:48 to 8:48   _____

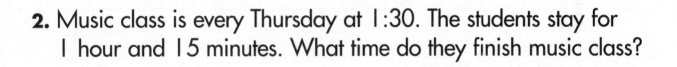

Time Word Problems

► Use your knowledge of time to solve the problems.

1. The bell rings for recess to begin at 12:15 and rings again at 1:00 for recess to end. Tamika volunteers to help her teacher water the classroom plants for the first 10 minutes of recess. How many minutes will she have left to play kickball when she is finished?

   _____

2. Music class is every Thursday at 1:30. The students stay for 1 hour and 15 minutes. What time do they finish music class?

   _____

3. Principal Allen is making up the schedule for next year. The winter holiday will be 2 weeks instead of the usual 10 days. Which is longer, two weeks or ten days? _____

4. Room 6 will take a school trip to the museum on April 5. The teacher must call 48 hours before arriving to confirm the time of the tour. On what date must she call? _____

5. The trip to the museum takes 1 hour. If the students have traveled for 35 minutes on the bus, how many more minutes will it be until they arrive? _____

Time Conversions

1 minute	= 60 seconds
1 hour	= 60 minutes
1 day	= 24 hours
1 week	= 7 days
1 month	= 28, 29, 30, or 31 days
1 year	= 365 days
	(366 during leap year)
1 decade	= 10 years

▶ Match equivalent values.

1.	3 decades	48 hours
2.	1 year (not a leap year)	90 seconds
3.	3 minutes	14 days
4.	half a day	31 days
5.	2 weeks	40 years
6.	half-hour	12 hours
7.	a minute and a half	180 seconds
8.	2 days	30 years
9.	one month	365 days
10.	4 decades	30 minutes

Perimeter

Perimeter—distance around an area.

▶ Find the perimeter of each figure below. Include the correct units in your answers.

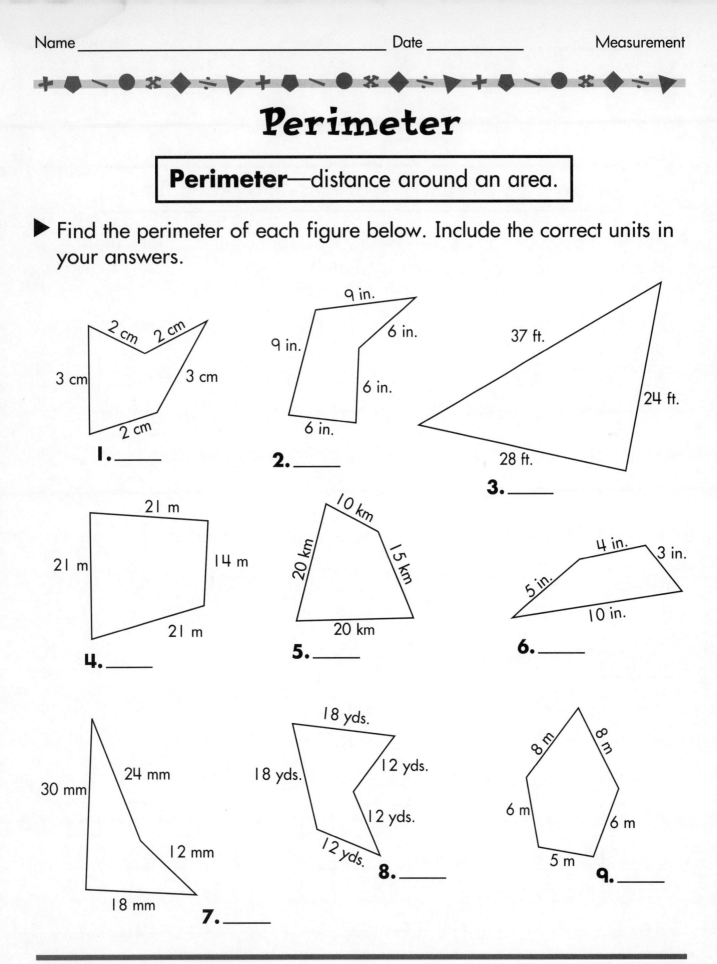

1. _____

2. _____

3. _____

4. _____

5. _____

6. _____

7. _____

8. _____

9. _____

0-7424-1721-2 Math

Area

Area—the amount of space inside a closed figure.

► Find the area of each figure below by counting the square units.
Each square measures 1 unit by 1 unit.

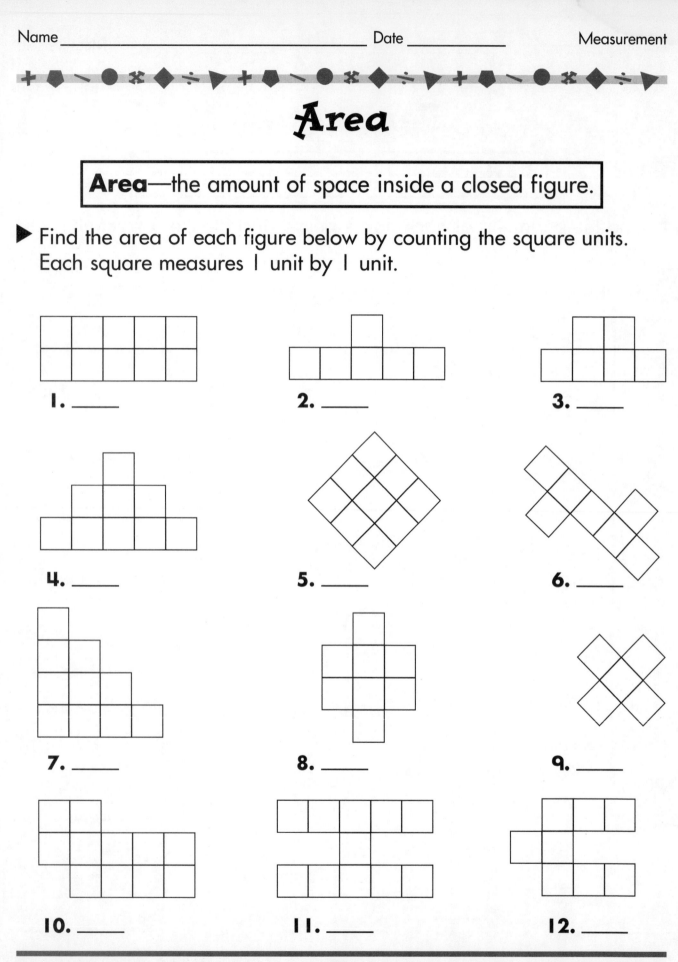

1. _____

2. _____

3. _____

4. _____

5. _____

6. _____

7. _____

8. _____

9. _____

10. _____

11. _____

12. _____

Area and Perimeter

▶ Use the clues to solve the puzzle.

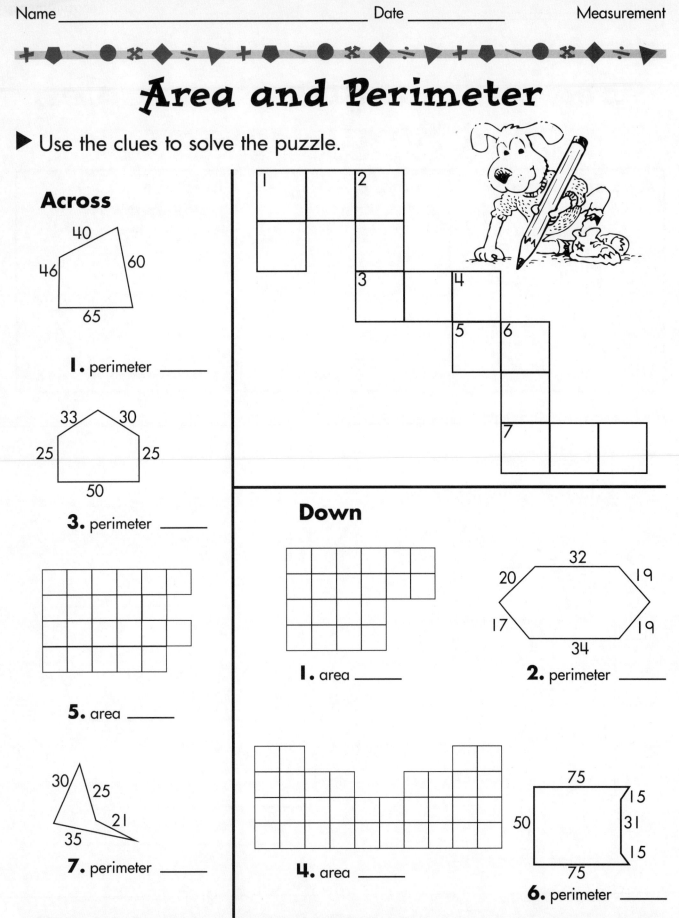

Across

1. perimeter _____

3. perimeter _____

5. area _____

7. perimeter _____

Down

1. area _____

2. perimeter _____

4. area _____

6. perimeter _____

Area of Triangles, Rectangles, and Parallelograms

Area of a triangle = 1/2 base x height	Area of a rectangle = length x width	Area of a parallelogram = base x height

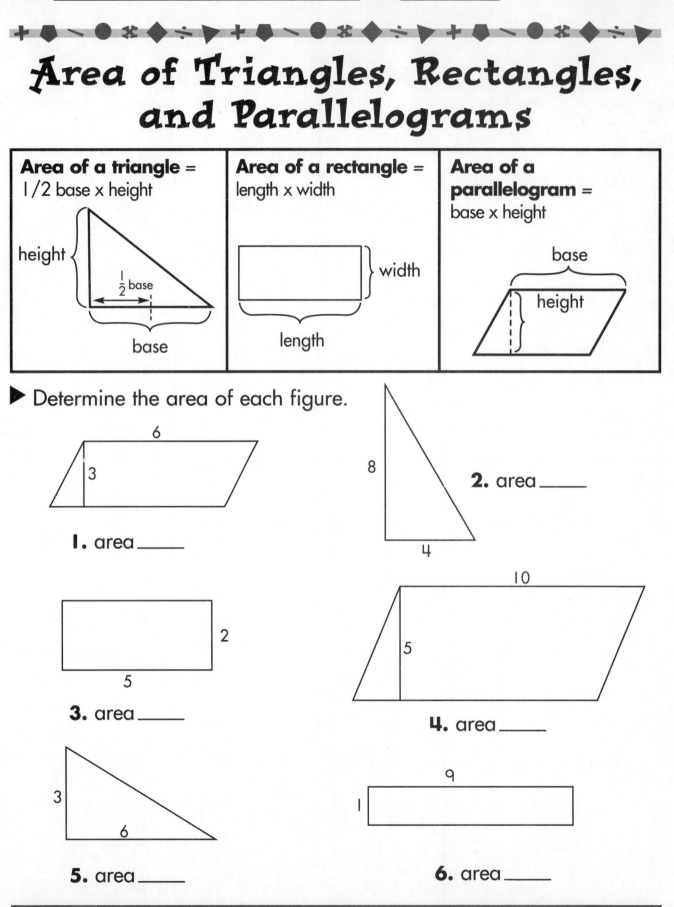

▶ Determine the area of each figure.

1. area _____

2. area _____

3. area _____

4. area _____

5. area _____

6. area _____

Estimating Area

You can estimate the area of an irregular shape by looking at the squares around it. In the example to the right, you know that 4 full squares are covered, so the area will be greater than 4 square units. You also know that the total figure is not larger than 16 square units (4 units x 4 units). You can estimate the area of the figure is between 4 and 16 square units.

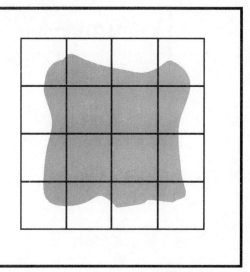

▶ For each of the following figures, estimate the area. Circle the number choice that is most likely the area (in square units) beneath each figure.

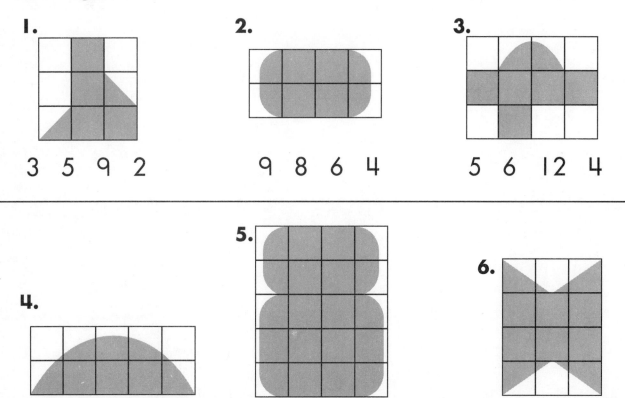

1.

3   5   9   2

2.

9   8   6   4

3.

5   6   12   4

4.

5   2   3   11

5.

20   9   23   14

6.

5   9   6   14

What Is Volume?

Volume—the amount of space inside a three-dimensional figure.

The volume of 1 cube is 1 cubic unit.

▶ Find the number of cubes and volume for each figure below.

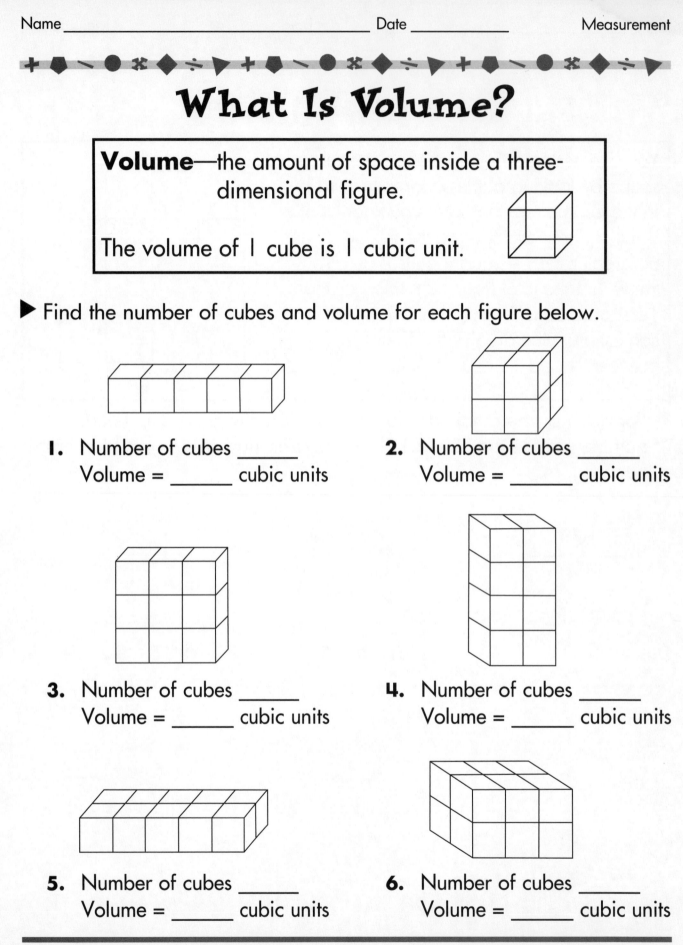

1. Number of cubes _____
Volume = _____ cubic units

2. Number of cubes _____
Volume = _____ cubic units

3. Number of cubes _____
Volume = _____ cubic units

4. Number of cubes _____
Volume = _____ cubic units

5. Number of cubes _____
Volume = _____ cubic units

6. Number of cubes _____
Volume = _____ cubic units

Find the Volume

► Find the volume by counting the number of blocks needed to make each shape. Record the volume in cubic units.

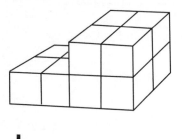

1. _____

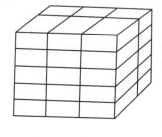

2. _____

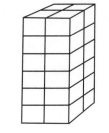

3. _____

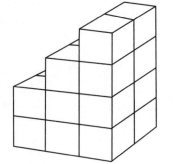

4. _____

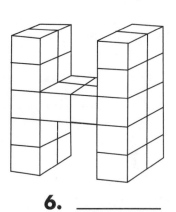

5. _____

6. _____

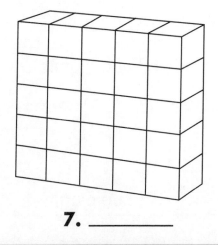

7. _____

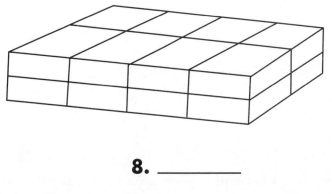

8. _____

Using a Rule to Find Volume

One way to find volume is to use the following rule:

Volume = length x **width** x **height**

▶ Use the formula to determine the volume of the figures below.
Match each figure to its correct volume.

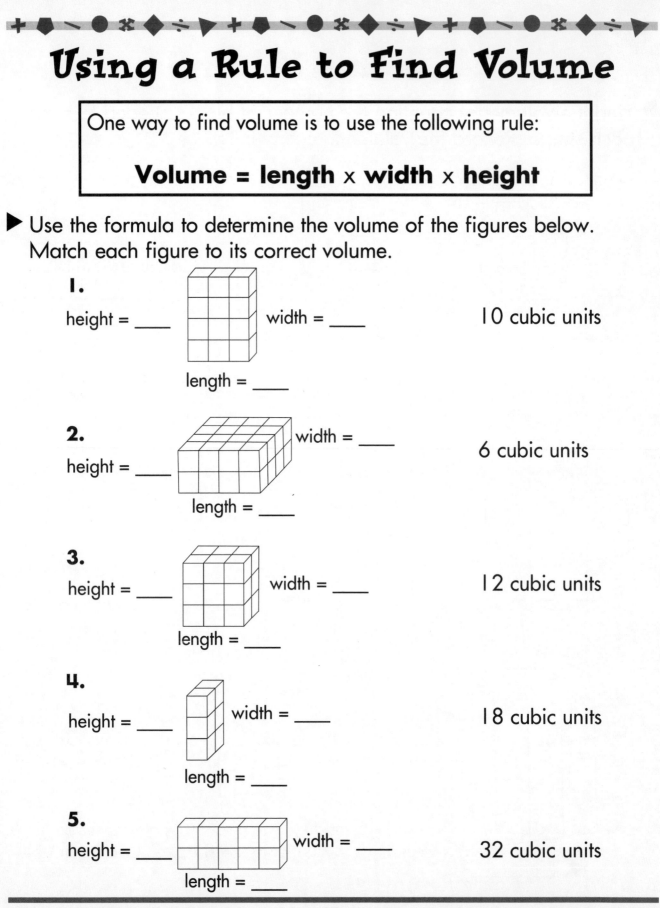

1.
height = ____   width = ____

length = ____

10 cubic units

2.
height = ____   width = ____

length = ____

6 cubic units

3.
height = ____   width = ____

length = ____

12 cubic units

4.
height = ____   width = ____

length = ____

18 cubic units

5.
height = ____   width = ____

length = ____

32 cubic units

Temperature

▶ Temperature can be measured in two ways. In the U.S. customary system, temperature is measured in degrees Fahrenheit (°F). In the metric system, temperature is measured in degrees Celsius (°C). The chart below compares some commonly used temperatures for both systems. Use the chart to help you answer the questions.

	Fahrenheit	Celsius
water boils	212°	100°
body temperature	98.6°	37°
room temperature	70°	20°
water freezes	32°	0°

1. When the students first arrived at school in the morning, the classroom thermometer read 67°F. By recess, it read 73°F. What was the temperature change? _____

2. Mary is not feeling well. Her mother takes her temperature. The thermometer shows a temperature of 101°F. Should Mary stay home today? _____

3. The water temperature at the ocean was 69°F in the morning. By the end of the day, there was a temperature change of 6° and the temperature was colder. What was the temperature at the end of the day? _____

4. What is the temperature difference between 15°F and 43°F? _____

5. On a warm summer day in Toronto, Canada, the temperature at noon was 28°C. By late evening, the temperature had dropped to 19°C. What was the temperature change? _____

6. Josh and Daniel want to play ice hockey. The outdoor rink is only open if the temperature is below freezing. The thermometer reads 2°C. Will the rink be open today? _____

Temperature

▶ Jason checked the thermometer outside his window at 3:00 P.M. every day for a week. The graph below represents his findings. Use the graph to solve the problems.

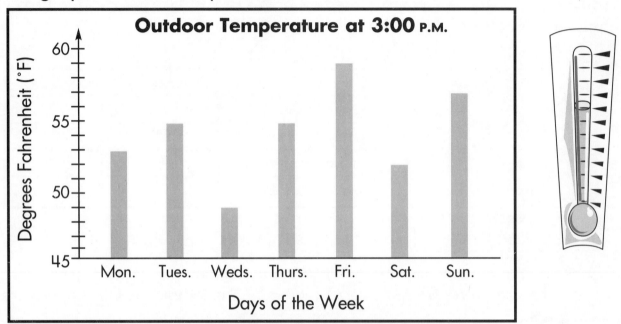

Outdoor Temperature at 3:00 P.M.

1. What was the high temperature for the week? _____
2. What was the low temperature for the week? _____
3. Which two days had the same temperature? _____
4. There was a temperature drop of 7 degrees from which day to which day? _____
5. What is the difference between the temperature on Wednesday and the temperature on Friday? _____
6. How many degrees difference is there between the temperature on Monday and the temperature on Sunday? _____
7. On which day would you be most likely to wear an extra jacket?

   _____
8. The temperature rose 2 degrees from which day to which day?

   _____

Measure Me

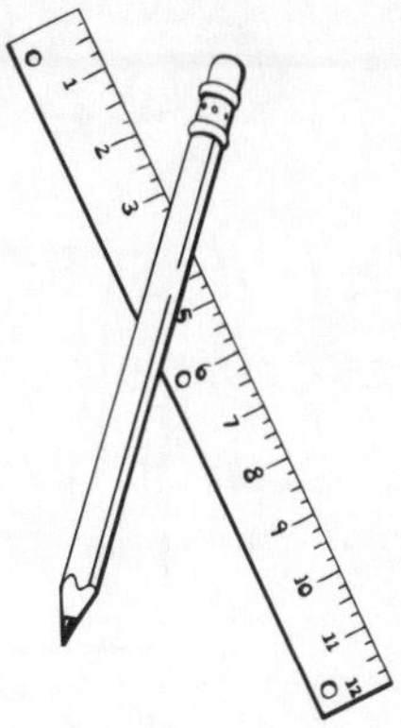

▶ Use a ruler to measure the following lines in inches.

1. _____

2. _____

3. _____

4. _____

5. _____

▶ Measure each line to the nearest centimeter.

6. _____

7. _____

8. _____

9. _____

10. _____

▶ Draw a line from the object to its approximate length.

1 centimeter

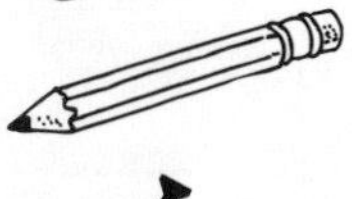

10 inches

18 centimeters

1.25 inches

2 inches

Customary Units of Length

| 1 foot = 12 inches |
| 1 yard = 3 feet |
| 1 mile = 5,280 feet |

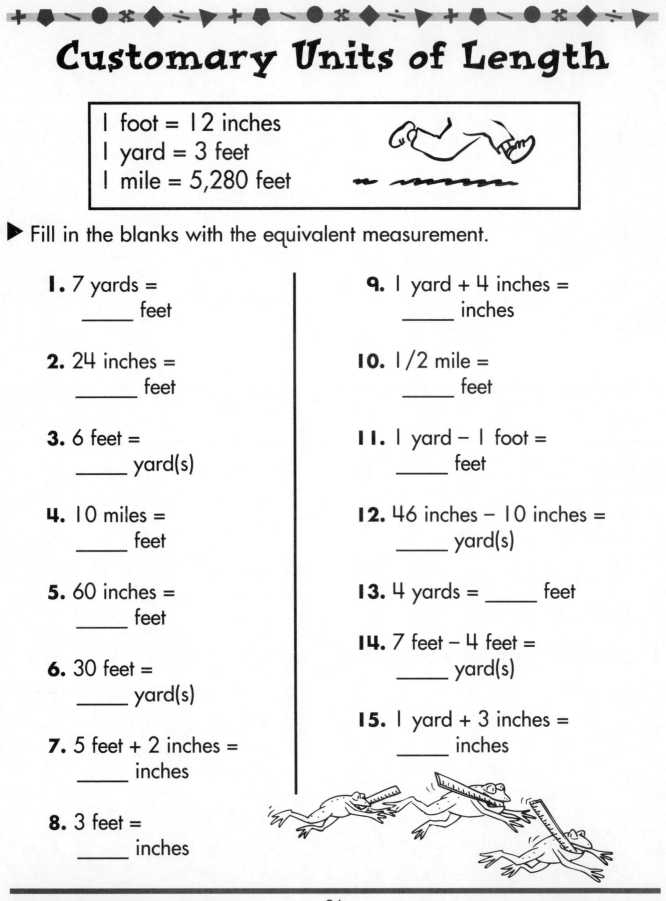

▶ Fill in the blanks with the equivalent measurement.

1. 7 yards =
_____ feet

2. 24 inches =
_____ feet

3. 6 feet =
_____ yard(s)

4. 10 miles =
_____ feet

5. 60 inches =
_____ feet

6. 30 feet =
_____ yard(s)

7. 5 feet + 2 inches =
_____ inches

8. 3 feet =
_____ inches

9. 1 yard + 4 inches =
_____ inches

10. 1/2 mile =
_____ feet

11. 1 yard − 1 foot =
_____ feet

12. 46 inches − 10 inches =
_____ yard(s)

13. 4 yards = _____ feet

14. 7 feet − 4 feet =
_____ yard(s)

15. 1 yard + 3 inches =
_____ inches

Metric Units of Length

▶ The metric measuring system is based on multiples of 10. Below is a chart of metric conversions.

1 centimeter (cm) = 10 millimeters (mm)
1 meter (m) = 100 centimeters (cm)
1 kilometer (km) = 1,000 meters (m)

1. Jodi measured her tomato plant. It is 34 centimeters. How many millimeters is this? _____

2. Meg has a plastic case that is 4 centimeters long. She found a shell that is 34 millimeters long. Will it fit in her case? _____

3. Kifa jumped 3 meters. How many centimeters is this?

_____

4. Jordan's desk is 1 meter by 1 meter. He would like to put his science project inside his desk. The science project is on poster board that is 95 centimeters by 110 centimeters. Will it fit inside his desk without sticking out? _____

5. Anna is walking in a 5-kilometer charity event. How many meters will she walk by the time she reaches the finish line?

_____

6. Jonathan is running in the 10,000-meter race. How many kilometers is the race? _____

Selecting Appropriate Units (Metric)

▶ Matching: Show which metric units would be best to measure these common items and events by writing the letter of the appropriate units next to each item. Each unit should be used only once.

___ 1. one apple
___ 2. short distance races
___ 3. liquid baby medicine
___ 4. amount of water in a water tower
___ 5. distance between cities
___ 6. height of a book
___ 7. a jug of milk
___ 8. towing capacity of a truck
___ 9. amount of medicine in a pill

a. meters
b. kilometers
c. centimeters
d. grams
e. milligrams
f. kilograms
g. liters
h. milliliters
i. kiloliters

▶ Common units of measurement are listed in the word bank below. Write each measurement in the appropriate spot on the grid below. There will be more than one word in each square.

Word Bank
grams
yards
meters
pounds
milliliters
centimeters
ounces
kilograms
quarts
inches
meters
kiloliters

	Mass	Capacity	Length
Metric			
Customary			

Customary Units of Capacity

1 tablespoon = 3 teaspoons
1 cup = 16 tablespoons = 8 fluid ounces
1 pint = 2 cups
1 quart = 2 pints
1 gallon = 4 quarts

▶ Find the following conversions. Show your work.

1. 18 pints = _____ quarts
2. 28 quarts = _____ pints
3. 10 pints = _____ cups
4. 18 cups = _____ quarts
5. 4 tablespoons = _____ teaspoons
6. 24 quarts = _____ gallons
7. 5 pints = _____ fluid ounces
8. 1 quart = _____ fluid ounces
9. 2 cups = _____ tablespoons

▶ Read the following problems and answer the questions.

10. Jackie drinks 1 pint of chocolate milk each day with her school lunch. How many cups of chocolate milk is that in 5 days? Does she drink enough in 5 days to fill a gallon?

11. Paula has a 20-gallon fish tank. She needs to treat the tank with a chemical. The directions say to put 1 drop in for every quart of water. How many drops of chemical are needed for this aquarium?

Metric Units of Capacity

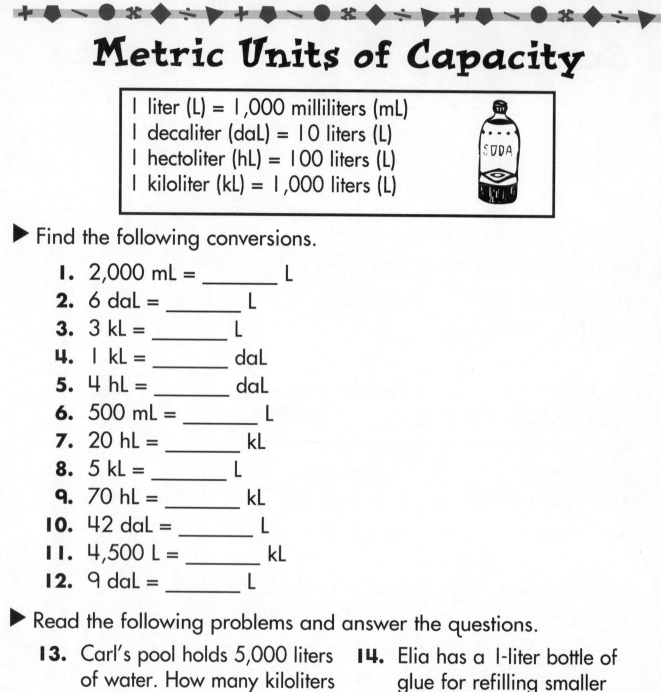

| 1 liter (L) = 1,000 milliliters (mL) |
| 1 decaliter (daL) = 10 liters (L) |
| 1 hectoliter (hL) = 100 liters (L) |
| 1 kiloliter (kL) = 1,000 liters (L) |

▶ Find the following conversions.

1. 2,000 mL = _____ L

2. 6 daL = _____ L

3. 3 kL = _____ L

4. 1 kL = _____ daL

5. 4 hL = _____ daL

6. 500 mL = _____ L

7. 20 hL = _____ kL

8. 5 kL = _____ L

9. 70 hL = _____ kL

10. 42 daL = _____ L

11. 4,500 L = _____ kL

12. 9 daL = _____ L

▶ Read the following problems and answer the questions.

13. Carl's pool holds 5,000 liters of water. How many kiloliters is this?

14. Elia has a 1-liter bottle of glue for refilling smaller bottles. The small bottle holds 200 milliliters. How many small bottles can she fill from the big one?

Selecting Appropriate Units
(Capacity)

▶ Circle the best unit of capacity for measuring the objects and containers below.

1.

mL   L   kL

2.

mL   L   kL

3.

mL   L   kL

4.

mL   L   kL

5.

mL   L   kL

6.

mL   L   kL

7.

mL   L   kL

8.

mL   L   kL

9.

mL   L   kL

10.

mL   L   kL

11.

mL   L   kL

12.

mL   L   kL

0-7424-1721-2 Math

Customary Units of Mass

| 1 pound (lb.) = 16 ounces (oz.) |
| 1 ton (t.) = 2,000 pounds (lbs.) |

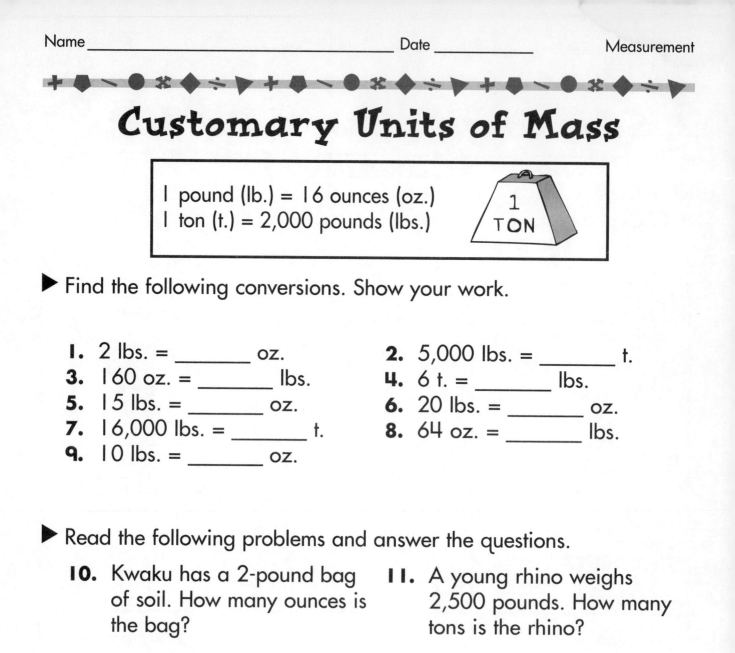

▶ Find the following conversions. Show your work.

1. 2 lbs. = _____ oz.

2. 5,000 lbs. = _____ t.

3. 160 oz. = _____ lbs.

4. 6 t. = _____ lbs.

5. 15 lbs. = _____ oz.

6. 20 lbs. = _____ oz.

7. 16,000 lbs. = _____ t.

8. 64 oz. = _____ lbs.

9. 10 lbs. = _____ oz.

▶ Read the following problems and answer the questions.

10. Kwaku has a 2-pound bag of soil. How many ounces is the bag?

11. A young rhino weighs 2,500 pounds. How many tons is the rhino?

12. A particular bridge has a weight capacity of 15 tons. A truck's loaded trailer weighs 40,000 pounds. Should the trucker drive over the bridge?

13. A recipe for apple pie calls for 2 pounds of apples. The produce scale says 34 ounces. Are there enough apples for a pie?

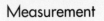

Metric Units of Mass

| 1 gram (g) = 1,000 milligrams (mg) |
| 1 kilogram (kg) = 1,000 grams (g) |
| 1 decagram (dag) = 10 kilograms (kg) |
| 1 hectogram (hg) = 100 kilograms (kg) |
| 1 metric ton (t) = 1,000 kilograms (kg) |

▶ Find the following conversions.

1. 10 kg = _____ g
2. 1 hg = _____ dag
3. 2,000 g = _____ kg
4. 500 g = _____ kg
5. 70 hg = _____ t
6. 2 g = _____ mg

7. 3 t = _____ kg
8. 4,500 g = _____ kg
9. 30 kg = _____ dag
10. 6,000 mg = _____ g
11. 4 dag = _____ kg
12. 500 kg = _____ hg

▶ Read the following problems and answer the questions.

13. Emilio has a bag of polished stones, each with a mass of 200 grams. How many stones are in the bag if the total mass equals 2 kilograms? _____

14. Tasha has a jar full of cookies with a mass of 175 grams. Each cookie weighs 5 grams. How many cookies are in the jar? _____

15. Kara has a collection of objects. Her plastic spider ring has a mass of 980 milligrams. A piece of quartz has a mass of 3 grams and a bag of buttons has a mass of 2,020 milligrams. What is the total mass of her collection in grams? _____

16. When Mark placed the green grapes on the scale, the mass was 200 grams short of 1 kilogram. He placed another 500 grams on the scale and decided to buy the whole bunch. How many grams in all did he purchase? _____

Selecting Appropriate Units (Mass)

▶ Choose grams (g) or kilograms (kg) to identify the appropriate unit of measurement.

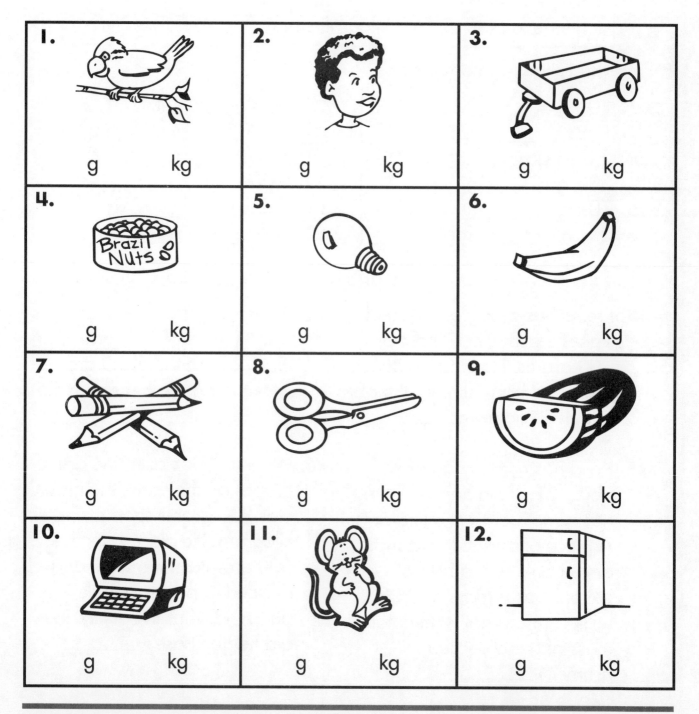

1.	2.	3.
g kg	g kg	g kg
4.	5.	6.
g kg	g kg	g kg
7.	8.	9.
g kg	g kg	g kg
10.	11.	12.
g kg	g kg	g kg

Pictograph

A **pictograph** uses a symbol or picture to represent numbers on a graph. The key will tell you the number that each picture represents. Use the pictograph below to answer the questions.

Votes for Class Trip

Place	Votes
Zoo	🧍🧍🧍┃
Museum	🧍🧍
Theater	🧍┃
Nature Center	🧍🧍┃

KEY
🧍 = 6 students
┃ = 3 students

▶ Use the pictograph to answer the questions below.

1. What is the total number of students who voted? _____

2. Which place received the least votes? _____

3. How many more students voted for the zoo than the theater? _____

4. Twelve students were absent the day of the vote. If 6 of them vote for the museum, and 6 of them vote for the theater, will that change the winning vote for the class trip? _____

5. Which place received the most votes? _____

Tally Chart

One way to organize data is to use a **tally chart**. One mark is used for each number, and a slash is drawn through every 4 marks to represent 5. The crossing guards are concerned that so many cars cross a street they do not monitor. They are using a tally chart to help present their findings to the principal.

▶ Answer the following questions based on the tally chart below.

1. What is the least number of cars that crossed Johnson Avenue? _____

2. What is the most number of cars that crossed Johnson Avenue? _____

3. Which day had the least number of cars? _____

4. What is the total number of cars that crossed from Monday through Friday?

_____

5. The principal may allow an extra crossing guard for one day of the week. Which day should the crossing guards recommend? _____

Number of Cars on Johnson Ave.
3:00 P.M. to 3:30 P.M.

Day	Tallies
Monday	卌 卌 卌 ||||
Tuesday	卌 卌 卌 |
Wednesday	卌 卌 卌 卌 ||
Thursday	卌 卌 ||||
Friday	卌 卌 卌 卌 卌 ||||

Venn Diagram

A **Venn diagram** is a unique way to compare data from multiple categories. The overlapping part of the circles is the place where multiple categories are true at the same time.

Name	Pizza Toppings
Irene	mushroom
David	pepperoni
Tamera	pepperoni, mushroom, extra cheese
Allison	mushroom, extra cheese
Jamal	pepperoni, mushroom
Pablo	pepperoni, extra cheese
Erin	mushroom, extra cheese
Tara	pepperoni
Chen	extra cheese
Larry	pepperoni, mushroom, extra cheese
Elizabeth	mushroom

▶ Use the data chart to help you write the names in the correct place on the Venn diagram.

Pepperoni

Mushroom

Extra Cheese

0-7424-1721-2 Math

Glyph

A **glyph** is a picture that represents data with several variables. Use the key to help you interpret the glyph below. Then create a glyph for yourself using the same key.

eyes	●● ▼▼	●● = boy ▼▼ = girl
mouth	⌣ ⌣	⌣ = eat lunch in cafeteria ⌣ = eat lunch from home
antennae		⌢⌢ = walk to school \／ = ride car to school \\／ = bus to school ⌇⌇ = ride bike to school
body	◯	number of body sections = number of month born
legs	♪♪♩♪	number of legs = number of people in family

▶ Using the glyph key, fill in the sentences below about the glyph below.

This person is a _____ with _____ people in his/her family.
To get to school, this person _____.
This person was born in the month of _____.
At lunchtime, this person eats _____.

Draw a bug glyph for yourself.

Circle Graph

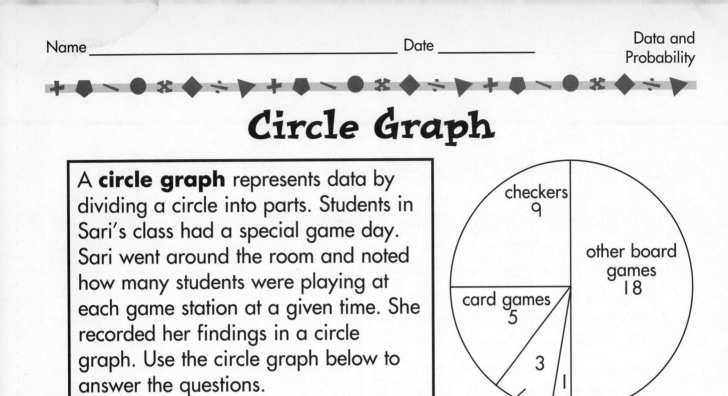

A **circle graph** represents data by dividing a circle into parts. Students in Sari's class had a special game day. Sari went around the room and noted how many students were playing at each game station at a given time. She recorded her findings in a circle graph. Use the circle graph below to answer the questions.

▶ Use the circle graph to answer the questions.

1. What is the total number of students in Sari's class that played on game day?_____

2. One game station was very popular, with half of the students playing there. Which station was it? _____

3. Which game station had the fewest players? _____

4. If Sari combined the dice games, card games, and chess stations, would that new group be larger, smaller, or the same size as the checkers group?

_____

5. Half as many students played checkers as played at which game station? _____

6. Sari's teacher needs to plan for next year's game day. Which game should she consider taking out? _____

Which two games should she be sure to include? _____

Line Graph

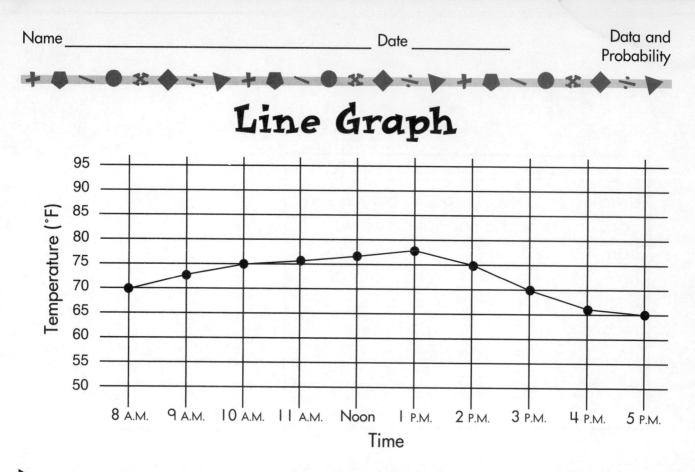

▶ Answer the questions about the graph above.

1. What can you say about the pattern of the temperature throughout the day? Explain why you think this pattern occurs. _____

_____

2. What is the difference in degrees between the temperature at 8 A.M. and 5 P.M.?_____

3. What is the highest temperature reached during the day?_____
At what time did this temperature occur? _____

4. What is the lowest temperature of the day? _____
At what time did this temperature occur? _____

5. Was the temperature change greater between 8 A.M. and 12 P.M. or between 1 P.M. and 5 P.M.? _____

Representing Data Different Ways

▶ The same data can be represented different ways depending on which style of chart is used. Use the information in the following table to fill in the bar chart and circle charts below.

School Election Results

Grade	Votes for Blue Party	Votes for Red Party	Total Votes by Grade
Third	25	5	30
Fourth	10	16	26
Fifth	15	21	36
Total Votes by Party	40	42	

School Election Results

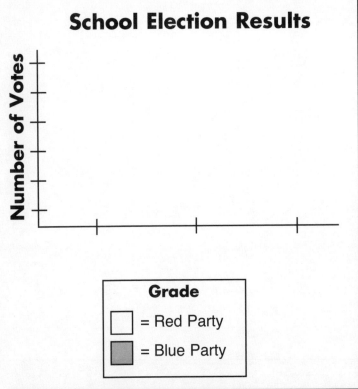

Number of Votes

Grade

☐ = Red Party

▨ = Blue Party

Blue Party by Grade

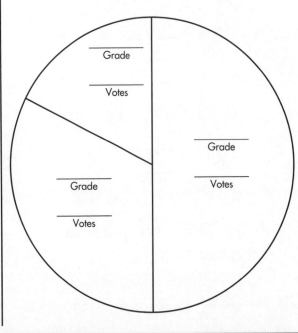

Grade

Votes

Grade

Votes

Grade

Votes

Median, Mode, and Range

The **median** is the number that is the number in the middle when a group of numbers is arranged in order from least to greatest.

Example:

20 25 26 26 26 26 **32** 33 34 34 35 37 39

The median is **32**.
The mode is **26**.
The range is **19**.

The **mode** is the number that occurs most often.

To find the **range**, subtract the least number from the greatest.

▶ For each of the following number groups, list the median, mode, and range. Hint: For some problems, you will need to rearrange the numbers in numerical order first.

1. 13 14 14 14 15 17 17 19 21
median _____
mode _____
range _____

2. 50 52 52 52 53 56 58 58 60
median _____
mode _____
range _____

3. 6 9 10 12 14 14 15
median _____
mode _____
range _____

4. 82 86 91 80 82 82 89
median _____
mode _____
range _____

5. 71 73 73 73 74 76 79
median _____
mode _____
range _____

6. 5 4 4 8 3 2 1
median _____
mode _____
range _____

7. 31 32 33 34 35 36 36
median _____
mode _____
range _____

8. 10 32 27 25 37 16 25
median _____
mode _____
range _____

Probable Outcomes

Probability is the degree to which something is likely or unlikely to happen. To find the probability, you need to know the total number of possibilities and the frequency of the unit in question.

▶ Look at the spinner. Answer the following questions.

1. What is the total number of possibilities for this spinner? _____

2. What is the probability of landing on a 7? _____

3. What is the probability of landing on an even number? _____

4. What is the probability of landing on a 6? _____

5. What is the probability of landing on an odd number? _____

▶ Various coins are placed in a bag. There are 2 quarters, 2 dimes, 1 nickel, and 3 pennies. One coin is drawn each turn. Answer the questions below.

6. What is the total number of possibilities for the bag? _____

7. Which coin is most likely to be drawn? _____

8. What is the probability of drawing a nickel? _____

9. What is the probability of drawing a quarter? _____

10. What is the probability of not drawing a dime? _____

Probable Outcomes

▶ Look at the spinner. What is the probability the arrow will land on—

1. a number? _____
2. an 8? _____
3. a circle? _____
4. a shape? _____
5. a triangle? _____

▶ Look at the spinner. What is the probability the arrow will land on—

6. a banana? _____
7. a fruit? _____
8. a star? _____
9. a triangle? _____
10. a square? _____

▶ Look at the spinner. What is the probability the arrow will land on—

11. a 5? _____
12. an odd number? _____
13. a triangle? _____
14. a 2? _____
15. a shape? _____

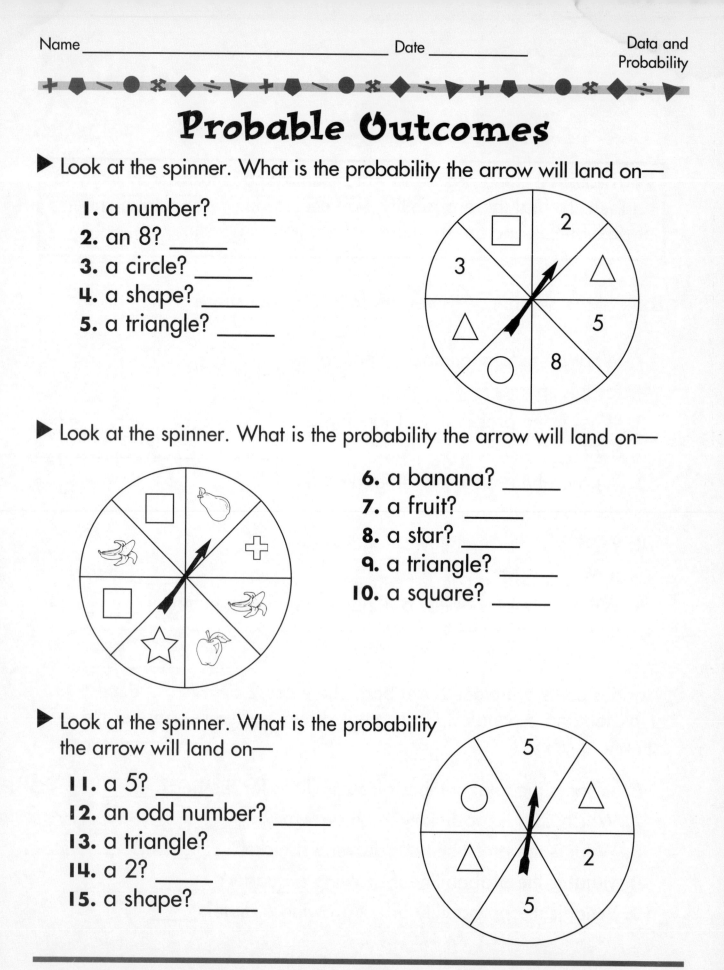

Relative Frequency

Relative Frequency states the actual frequency of an event related to the total number possible.

Classroom Survey	
Groups	**Out of 24 Students**
Boys	11
Girls	13
Girls with tennis shoes	4
Girls with sandals	9
Boys with tennis shoes	6
Boys with sandals	5

▶ Using the chart above, find the following relative frequencies compared to the whole class.

1. Boys with sandals _____5 out of 24, or 5/24_____

2. Girls with sandals _____

3. Girls with tennis shoes _____

4. Boys with tennis shoes _____

5. Students with sandals _____

6. Students with tennis shoes _____

7. Boys in the classroom _____

8. Girls in the classroom _____

9. Boys and girls in the classroom _____

10. Girls with dress shoes _____

Degree of Likelihood

▶ Melanie put 3 yellow buttons, 6 red buttons, 2 blue buttons, and 1 green button into a bag. Mikel draws one button out of the bag each time. Answer the questions below.

I. What is the chance that Mikel will pull out each color?

yellow _____ chance out of _____
blue _____ chance out of _____
red _____ chance out of _____
green _____ chance out of _____

2. Which color is Mikel most likely to pull out? _____
Which color is Mikel least likely to pull out? _____

3. If Melanie wanted to make the chance of getting a blue button even with the chance of getting a green button, what should she do?_____

4. If Melanie wanted each button to have an equal chance of being drawn, what could she do?

_____

5. If Mikel were to pull out a yellow button on his first turn and keep it out of the bag, what will the chance be for each color on his next turn?

yellow _____ chance out of _____
blue _____ chance out of _____
red _____ chance out of _____
green _____ chance out of _____

Degree of Likelihood

▶ The Room 3 students at Westfield Elementary are bored with their lunches. They decide to hold a lunch surprise day. They put their sandwiches in one pile and their snacks in another. Each student will be blindfolded and then choose one sandwich and one snack from each table. Using the information below, answer the questions.

Sandwich Type	Number
tuna	3
jelly	2
turkey	5
cheese	4
chicken salad	1

Snack Type	Number
cookie	6
carrot sticks	2
chips	3
banana	2
apple	2

1. If all the snacks are still on the table, what is the probability of a student choosing a cookie as a snack? _____

2. What is the probability of getting a cookie after 2 cookies have been chosen? _____

3. If all the sandwiches are still on the table, what is the probability of choosing a turkey sandwich? _____

4. If all the snacks are still on the table, what is the probability of choosing a fruit? _____

5. Most of the students have chosen by the time it is Ray's turn. There are 3 sandwiches left—chicken salad, turkey, and tuna. What is the probability that Ray will choose turkey? _____

Place Value............Page 4

1. 54,671—seven tens
2. 354,942—nine hundreds
3. 203,203—two hundred thousands
4. 67,881—seven thousands
5. 495,463—six tens
6. 485,751—eight ten thousands
7. 763,389—three hundreds
8. 892,855—five ones
9. 103,254—one hundred thousand

Place Value............Page 5

Millions			Thousands					
2	9	5,	1	0	6,	3	8	4

1. 4
2. 3
3. 8
4. 9
5. 4
6. 8
7. 0

Place Value............page 6

Across
1. 751
4. 285
5. 908
7. 678
10. 65
11. 83
12. 741
14. 257
15. 523
18. 495

Down
1. seven hundred twenty-eight
2. fifty-eight
3. one hundred fifty-six
5. nine hundred sixty-seven
6. fifty-four
8. seven hundred eighty-five
9. eight hundred thirty-seven
13. one hundred fifty-four
14. two hundred thirty-five
16. twenty-nine

Rounding............page 7

Tens
16→20   32→30   58→60
75→80   92→90   82→80
27→30   54→50   66→70

Hundreds
921→900   662→700   882→900
458→500   187→200   363→400
393→400   527→500   211→200

Thousands
2,495→2,000   3,379→3,000

7,001→7,000   8,821→9,000
5,111→5,000   9,339→9,000

4,289→4,000
6,213→6,000
2,985→3,000

Addition ....page 8

1. 39
2. 59
3. 55
4. 68
5. 96
6. 88
7. 78
8. 77
9. 87
10. 99
11. 53
12. 77

Addition ....page 9

1. 82
2. 51
3. 77
4. 96
5. 52
6. 73
7. 92
8. 60

Addition ....page 10

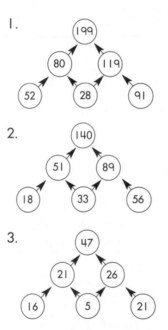

Addition ....page 11

1. 481
2. 786
3. 691
4. 884
5. 980
6. 987
7. 391
8. 872
9. 793
10. 844
11. 994
12. 792

Addition ....page 12

What do you call a bull that's asleep? A bulldozer.

563 + 156 = 719 (A)
484 + 293 = 777 (B)
256 + 381 = 637 (U)
595 + 241 = 836 (L)
352 + 484 = 836 (L)
254 + 291 = 545 (D)
375 + 381 = 756 (O)
285 + 124 = 409 (Z)
558 + 191 = 749 (E)
466 + 262 = 728 (R)

Addition ....page 13

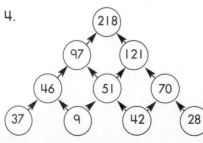

Addition ....page 14

1. 126
2. 173
3. 185
4. 190
5. 263
6. 182
7. 243
8. 203
9. 143
10. 241
11. 215
12. 133

Addition Problem Solving ....page 15

1. 1,054
2. 461
3. 1,419
4. 18 blocks
5. 15
6. Answers may vary.
   $12.00 + $6.00 + $6.00 = $24.00

Subtraction ....page 16

1. 69   7. 38
2. 16   8. 44
3. 19   9. 28
4. 27   10. 12
5. 12   11. 46
6. 28   12. 79

Subtraction ....page 17

Center MATHO card wins;
diagonally from bottom left to
upper right.

1. 38   9. 186
2. 49   10. 39
3. 143   11. 819
4. 25   12. 939
5. 259   13. 63
6. 405   14. 116
7. 211   15. 414
8. 69

Subtraction ....page 18

1. 468   7. 486
2. 369   8. 266
3. 264   9. 184
4. 688   10. 264
5. 89   11. 187
6. 149   12. 565

Subtraction ....page 19

1. 266   7. 491
2. 454   8. 63
3. 397   9. 273
4. 262   10. 693
5. 394   11. 281
6. 188   12. 445

Subtraction ....Page 20

What has four legs and flies?

A picnic table.

1. 165 (A)   7. 156 (C)
2. 368 (P)   8. 349 (T)
3. 656 (I)   9. 165 (A)
4. 156 (C)   10. 277 (B)
5. 789 (N)   11. 164 (L)
6. 656 (I)   12. 189 (E)

Subtraction ....Page 21

1. 233   7. 264
2. 216   8. 360
3. 418   9. 149
4. 112   10. 438
5. 129   11. 102
6. 493   12. 165

Subtraction ....Page 22

1. 4,137   8. 3,732
2. 288   9. 179
3. 371   10. 186
4. 3,648   11. 1,991
5. 2,779   12. 2,544
6. 2,777   13. 2,514
7. 146   14. 4,107

2,514	288	186	3,732	4,107
	2,779	156	1,901	2,414	4,137
3,748	3,337	2,777	371	179	1,991
3,048	3,737	146	2,717		
679	237	2,544	3,648		

Subtraction Problem Solving ....page 23

Team One

	Sit-Ups	Push-Ups	Jumping Jacks	Meters Run
Total	91	82	83	1,500

Team Two

	Sit-Ups	Push-Ups	Jumping Jacks	Meters Run
Total	82	84	88	1,750

1. 18
2. 32
3. Team Two
4. Team Two

Multiplication.......page 24

1. 12   4. 9
2. 10   5. 14
3. 5   6. 8

Multiplication.......page 25

1. 54   11. 56
2. 15   12. 28
3. 48   13. 16
4. 18   14. 25
5. 42   15. 63
6. 30   16. 27
7. 24
8. 72
9. 16
10. 24

Multiplication.......page 26

x	0	1	2	3	4	5	6	7	8	9
0	0	0	0	0	0	0	0	0	0	0
1	0	1	2	3	4	5	6	7	8	9
2	0	2	4	6	8	10	12	14	16	18
3	0	3	6	9	12	15	18	21	24	27
4	0	4	8	12	16	20	24	28	32	36
5	0	5	10	15	20	25	30	35	40	45
6	0	6	12	18	24	30	36	42	48	54
7	0	7	14	21	28	35	42	49	56	63
8	0	8	16	24	32	40	48	56	64	72
9	0	9	18	27	36	45	54	63	72	81

Multiplication.......page 27

1. 21   7. 14
2. 30   8. 18
3. 6   9. 36
4. 24   10. 24
5. 18   11. 10
6. 32   12. 27

Multiplication.......page 28

1. 25   9. 10
2. 21   10. 35
3. 18   11. 81
4. 56   12. 40
5. 63   13. 30
6. 36   14. 72
7. 45   15. 24
8. 42   16. 28

Multiplication.......page 29

1. 594   9. 1,862
2. 308   10. 912
3. 1,430   11. 3,416
4. 931   12. 1,440
5. 1,176   13. 3,108
6. 540   14. 6,664
7. 1,050   15. 2,380
8. 703

Answer Key

Multiplication.......page 30

All answers are clockwise beginning with shaded box.

Top dartboard: 1,054, 1,768, 2,686, 1,462, 918, 2,108.
Total = 9,996

Middle dartboard: 1,508, 1,118, 2,418, 1,248, 1,404, 910
Total = 8,606

Bottom dartboard: 2,208, 3,450, 2,806, 2,714, 3,910, 1,472.
Total = 16,560

Multiplication.......page 31

Row 1	Row 2
32,296 (A)	64,790 (G)
5,486 (J)	35,392 (O)
55,800 (A)	35,476 (E)
37,884 (B)	57,672 (D)
19,912 (U)	39,648 (!)

Row 3
22,815 (B)
41,610 (U)
67,824 (E)
24,414 (N)
45,408 (O)

Multiplication Problem Solving.......page 32

1. 48
2. 120
3. 36
4. 85
5. 60
6. $70.00

Division.......page 33

1. 21 ÷ 7
2. 24 ÷ 3
3. 27 ÷ 9
4. 48 ÷ 8
5. 18 ÷ 9
6. 45 ÷ 5
7. 42 ÷ 7
8. 56 ÷ 8
9. 49 ÷ 7
10. 63 ÷ 7
11. 36 ÷ 6
12. 40 ÷ 8

Division.......page 34

1. 4
2. 3
3. 7
4. 6
5. 4
6. 4
7. 2
8. 6
9. 9
10. 4

Division.......page 35

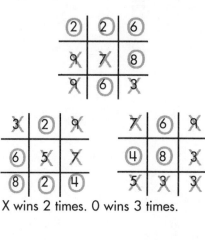

X wins 2 times. 0 wins 3 times.

Division.......page 36

1. 5 R3
2. 4 R3
3. 3 R2
4. 6 R3
5. 8 R2
6. 9 R1
7. 8 R3
8. 7 R2
9. 5 R3
10. 6 R5
11. 4 R5
12. 6 R3

Division.......page 37

1. 8, Rule 1
2. 4, Rule 1
3. 0, Rule 3
4. Not possible, Rule 4
5. 1, Rule 2
6. 0, Rule 3
7. Not possible, Rule 4
8. 1, Rule 2

Division.......page 38

1. 18 R2 (18 x 3)
2. 21 R1 (21 x 3)
3. 92 (92 x 3)
4. 42 R1 (42 x 3)
5. 59 R1 (59 x 3)
6. 58 R1 (58 x 3)
7. 78 R2 (78 x 3)
8. 10 R2 (10 x 3)
9. 28 R2 (28 x 3)
10. 82 R1 (82 x 3)

Division.......page 39

1. 168 R3
7. 874

2. 264 R2
3. 213 R1
4. 748 R2
5. 663 R1
6. 441 R6
8. 747 R1
9. 149
10. 422 R2
11. 796 R7
12. 691 R5

Division.......page 40

Visitor team wins.
1. 39
2. 31 R6
3. 73
4. 43
5. 23 R1
6. 31 R7
7. 42 R3
8. 64 R11

Division Problem Solving.......page 41

1. 30 ÷ 5 = 6
2. 4 per family member, 4 for scrapbook; 24 ÷ 5 = 4R4
3. 16
4. 9
5. 4

Mixed Operations.......page 42

1. 2
2. 100
3. 0
4. 18
Total treasure: 120

Mixed Operations.......page 43

x	6	2	4	7	1
5	30	10	20	35	5
8	48	16	32	56	8
3	18	6	12	21	3
9	54	18	36	63	9

−	82	53	41	54	62
16	66	37	25	38	46
21	61	32	20	33	41
18	64	35	23	36	44
32	50	21	9	22	30

+	23	15	31	89	58
19	42	34	50	108	77
57	80	72	88	146	115
63	86	78	94	152	121
45	68	60	76	136	103

x	6	3	8	4	1
4	24	12	32	16	4
9	54	27	72	36	9
5	30	15	40	20	5
7	42	21	56	28	7

÷ was not used.

Averaging ....page 44

1. 93 (E)
2. 53 (A)
3. 91 (D)
4. 410 (C)
5. 190 (B)
6. 83 (G)
7. 55 (F)
8. 262 (J)
9. 89 (K)
10. 3 (I)
11. 33 (H)
12. 521 (O)
13. 90 (N)
14. 8 (M)
15. 94 (L)

Averaging ....page 45

What is purple and goes thump, thump? A grape with a flat tire.

1. 23
2. 86
3. 38
4. 17
5. 47
6. 49
7. 11
8. 35
9. 67
10. 39
11. 76
12. 8

Fractions ....page 46

1. $\frac{2}{3} > \frac{1}{3}$
2. $\frac{1}{4} < \frac{5}{8}$
3. $\frac{3}{8} < \frac{2}{3}$
4. $\frac{3}{4} > \frac{1}{6}$
5. $\frac{2}{7} < \frac{4}{7}$
6. $\frac{2}{8} < \frac{1}{2}$
7. $\frac{4}{9} < \frac{2}{3}$
8. $\frac{3}{6} > \frac{1}{4}$
9. $\frac{3}{4} < \frac{4}{5}$

Fractions ....page 47

1. $\frac{2}{4} = \frac{4}{8}$
2. $\frac{1}{3} = \frac{2}{6}$
3. $\frac{1}{3} = \frac{3}{9}$
4. $\frac{3}{4} = \frac{6}{8}$
5. $\frac{1}{4} = \frac{3}{12}$
6. $\frac{1}{2} = \frac{3}{6}$
7. $\frac{1}{3} = \frac{4}{12}$
8. $\frac{1}{3} = \frac{5}{15}$
9. $\frac{2}{3} = \frac{4}{6}$
10. $\frac{1}{2} = \frac{6}{12}$

Fractions ....page 48

Answers are clockwise beginning at shaded box.

Snowman body (center):
$\frac{2}{5}$ $\frac{5}{5}$ $\frac{9}{16}$ $\frac{5}{16}$ $\frac{12}{16}$

$\frac{10}{16}$ $\frac{4}{5}$ $\frac{3}{5}$

Snowman body (bottom):
$\frac{3}{4}$ $\frac{2}{4}$ $\frac{4}{4}$ $\frac{11}{18}$ $\frac{14}{18}$ $\frac{12}{18}$

$\frac{5}{7}$ $\frac{6}{7}$ $\frac{4}{7}$ $\frac{7}{8}$ $\frac{5}{8}$ $\frac{3}{8}$

Broom:
$\frac{5}{9}$ $\frac{7}{9}$ $\frac{6}{9}$ $\frac{8}{9}$

Fractions ....page 49

What kind of beans will not grow in a garden? Jelly beans.

1. $\frac{5}{8}$
2. $\frac{2}{4}$
3. $\frac{3}{7}$
4. $\frac{3}{6}$
5. $\frac{6}{12}$
6. $\frac{7}{16}$
7. $\frac{3}{5}$
8. $\frac{4}{10}$

Fractions ....page 50

How do you spell mousetrap with just 4 letters? A cat.

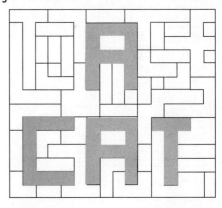

Decimals ....page 51

1. .7
2. .6
3. .8
4. .9
5. .1
6. .5
7. Any four sections shaded.
8. Any three sections shaded.
9. Any two sections shaded.

Decimals ....page 52

1. 9.4
2. 7.8
3. 10.9
4. 7.9
5. 6.9
6. 2.7
7. 1.1
8. 5.3
9. 2.5
10. 2.4
11. .48
12. .59
13. .68
14. .79
15. .99

Money ....page 53

1. $0.37 (3 dimes, 1 nickel, 2 pennies)
2. $1.90 (3 half-dollars, 2 dimes, 4 nickels)
3. $0.37 (1 quarter, 1 dime, 2 pennies)
4. $1.14 (2 half-dollars, 2 nickels, 4 pennies)
5. $1.92 (6 quarters, 4 dimes, 2 pennies)
6. $3.30 (5 half-dollars, 2 quarters, 3 dimes)

Money ....page 54

produce	total cost	change back
apples	$4.10	$0.90
blueberries	$2.01	$0.24
broccoli	$3.64	$1.36
cantaloupe	$6.64	$3.36
carrots	$0.81	$0.19
cucumbers	$2.16	$0.84
green beans	$0.96	$0.04
kiwi	$3.30	$1.70
peaches	$8.82	$1.18
pears	$3.12	$1.88
strawberries	$4.65	$0.35
tomatoes	$6.02	$3.98

Shape Patterns ....page 55

1. triangle
2. square
3. hexagon
4. large circle
5. pentagon

Number Patterns ....page 56

1, 3, 5, **7**, **9**, 11, 13 (Rule +2)

70, **60**, 50, **40**, **30**, 20, 10 (Rule −10)

1, 8, 15, 22, **29**, **36**, **43** (Rule +7)

36, 33, 30, **27**, **24**, **21**, **18** (Rule −3)

115, 100, 85, **70**, **55**, **40**, **25** (Rule −15)

64, 55, 46, **37**, **28**, **19**, **10** (Rule −9)

17, 25, 33, **41**, **49**, **57**, **65** (Rule +8)

96, **90**, 84, 78, **72**, **66**, **60** (Rule −6)

88, **77**, 66, **55**, 44, **33**, **22** (Rule −11)

12, 24, 36, **48**, **60**, **72**, **84** (Rule +12)

Number Patterns ....page 57

25 squares have circles.
7 squares have both a circle and an X.

1	**2**	3	**4**	**5**	6	**7**	**8**	9	10
2	4	**6**	**8**	10	**12**	**14**	16	**18**	20
3	**6**	**9**	12	**15**	**18**	21	**24**	**27**	30
4	**8**	12	**16**	**20**	24	**28**	**32**	36	40
5	10	**15**	**20**	25	**30**	**35**	40	**45**	50
6	**12**	**18**	24	**30**	**36**	42	**48**	**54**	60
7	**14**	21	**28**	**35**	42	**49**	**56**	63	70
8	16	**24**	**32**	40	**48**	**56**	64	**72**	80
9	**18**	**27**	36	**45**	**54**	63	**72**	**81**	90
10	**20**	30	**40**	**50**	60	**70**	**80**	**90**	100

Missing Values ....page 58

1. 7 **+** 3 = 10
2. 15 **+** 5 = 20
3. 13 **−** 7 = 6
4. 3 **x** 2 = 6
5. 4 **x** 2 = 8
6. 12 **−** 6 = 6
7. 23 **+** 3 = 26
8. 10 **÷** 5 = 2
9. 49 **+** 19 = 68
10. 21 **−** 4 = 17
11. 12 **x** 2 = 24
12. 19 **+** 3 = 22
13. 17 **−** 7 = 10
14. 3 **+** 18 = 21
15. 2 **x** 5 = 10
16. 7 **x** 6 = 42
17. 32 **−** 4 = 28
18. 16 **÷** 4 = 4
19. 5 **+** 6 = 11
20. 31 **−** 1 = 30

Missing Values ....page 59

1. 14 + **3** = 10 + 7
2. 10 x 1 = **7** + 3
3. 8 + 3 + **3** = 10 + 4
4. 3 x **2** = 10 − 4
5. **3** + 2 = 10 − 5
6. 11 x **1** = 6 + 5
7. 7 + 3 = **6** + 4
8. **7** + 1 = 4 x 2
9. 18 + 27 = 15 + **30**
10. **7** x 3 = 19 + 2
11. 10 + 3 = **16** − 3
12. 8 ÷ **2** = 4 x 1
13. **20** − 5 = 7 + 8
14. 9 ÷ **3** = 1 + 2
15. 37 − **5** = 18 + 14
16. **20** ÷ 2= 13 − 3
17. 4 + 4 = **16** − 8
18. 7 ÷ **1** = 5 + 2
19. 16 + **14** = 21 + 9
20. **8** = 64 ÷ 8

Number Letters ....page 60

1. m = 26
2. a = 16
3. s = 58
4. t = 38
5. u = 31
6. o = 19
7. b = 20
8. f = 73
9. e = 40
10. d = 52
11. r = 23
12. l = 22
13. n = 42
14. g = 18
15. c = 17

Message: Number letters don't scare me!

Number Pyramids ....page 61

1.

```
      21
   13     8
  6    7    1
```

2.

```
            42
         19    23
        8    11   12
       5    3    8    4
```

3.

```
              63
           30    33
         15    15    18
        10    5    10    8
       9    1    4    6    2
```

4.

```
        21
     10    11
    2    8    3
```

5.

```
           45
        28    17
       17   11    6
      7    10    1    5
```

6.

```
            88
         42    46
       19    23    23
      7    12    11    12
     4    3    9    2    10
```

7.

```
                344
             164    180
           77    87    93
         35    42    45    48
       14    21    21    24    24
      4    10    11    10    14    10
     1    3    7    4    6    8    2
```

Find the Rule........page 62

IN	78	15	41	22	37	**16**	55
OUT	65	2	28	**9**	**24**	3	**42**

Rule: **-13**

IN	2	9	81	76	37	**25**	**42**
OUT	11	18	**90**	85	**48**	34	51

Rule: **+ 9**

IN	82	16	70	34	44	**50**	60
OUT	41	8	**35**	**17**	22	25	**30**

Rule: **÷ 2**

Pre-Algebra Problem Solving ....page 63

Third Grade
C = 14
S = 7
V = 4

Fourth Grade
C = 16
S = 16
V = 0

Fifth Grade
C = 8
S = 16
V = 4

Total Votes for All Grades
C = 38
S = 39
V = 8

What's a Polygon? ....page 64

1. Polygons are closed figures with straight sides.
2. A shape that is open or has curved sides is not a polygon.

Types of Triangle ....page 65

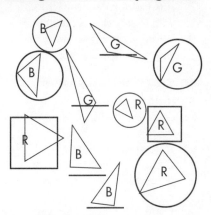

Quadrilaterals .....page 66

1. rhombus
2. rectangle
3. trapezoid
4. quadrilateral
5. square
6. parallelogram
7. quadrilateral
8. trapezoid

Types of Polygons ....page 67

1. f. octagon
2. c. pentagon
3. a. triangle
4. b. quadrilateral
5. d. hexagon
6. b. quadrilateral
7. d. hexagon
8. g. not a polygon (curved sides)
9. e. heptagon
10. g. not a polygon (curved sides)

Identifying Polygons ....page 68

1. octagon—polygon with 8 sides
2. square—quadrilateral with 4 right angles and 4 equal sides
3. trapezoid—quadrilateral with 1 set of parallel sides
4. equilateral triangle—triangle with 3 equal sides
5. rectangle—quadrilateral with 4 right angles and opposite sides of equal length

0-7424-1721-2 Math

6. pentagon—polygon with 5 sides
7. parallelogram—quadrilateral with 2 sets of parallel sides
8. isosceles triangle—triangle with 2 equal sides

Dimensions .... page 69

1. rectangle
2. octagon, rectangle
3. triangle
4. square
5. circle
6. pentagon, rectangle

Pyramids and Prisms .... page 70

1. prism
2. neither
3. pyramid
4. pyramid
5. prism
6. neither
7. prism
8. pyramid
9. prism

Cones, Cylinders, and Spheres .... page 71

1. cylinder
2. sphere
3. cone
4. none of these
5. sphere
6. sphere
7. cylinder
8. cone
9. none of these
10. cone
11. none of these
12. sphere

Classifying Prisms .... page 72

1. Group 1: Circled shape has a pentagon for a base and others have rectangular bases.
   Group 2: Circled shape has a hexagon for a base and others have triangular bases.
   Group 3: Circled shape has rectangular base and others have hexagonal bases.
2. Group 1: Rectangular bases

Group 2: Triangular bases
Group 3: Hexagonal bases

Congruent or Similar? .... page 73

1. similar
2. congruent
3. neither
4. similar
5. congruent
6. neither
Students will draw shapes to match in a size either smaller or larger than the one shown.

Symmetry .... page 74

1. yes
2. no
3. yes
4. no
Students will draw shapes to match. Words at the bottom are DECK, TOM, and MAYA.

Reflection and Rotation .... page 75

1. rotation
2. reflection
3. reflection
4. rotation
5. rotation
6. reflection

Lines, Line Segments and Rays .... page 76

1. d
2. c
3. e
4. a
5. b

Parts of a Circle ... page 77

1. radius, radius
2. diameter, diameter
3. chord, radius
4. chord, chord
5. chord, diameter
6. radius, radius

Coordinate Graphing .... page 78

1. acorn   (2, 3)
2. frog   (3, 3)
3. worm   (5, 4)
4. lily pad (3, 5)

5. boat   (6, 1)
6. picnic basket (4, 2)
7. rock   (5, 7)
8. butterfly   (0, 4)
9. flower   (2, 6)
10. leaf   (1, 7)
11. fish   (1, 4)
12. bird   (6, 6)

Using a Grid .... page 79

1. 7 miles
2. 5 miles
3. 10 miles
4. 17 miles

Using a Grid .... page 80

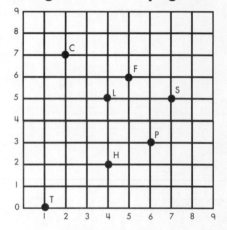

Types of Angles ... page 81

1. right angle
2. obtuse angle
3. obtuse angle
4. acute angle
5. obtuse angle
6. acute angle
7. obtuse angle
8. right angle
9. obtuse angle
10. right angle
11. acute angle
12. acute angle

Time Angles ....page 82

1.	90°	11.	90°
2.	180°	12.	90°
3.	360°	13.	360°
4.	270°	14.	90°
5.	180°	15.	180°
6.	180°	16.	270°
7.	180°	17.	90°
8.	270°	18.	90°
9.	270°	19.	270°
10.	180°	20.	360°

Time Word Problems ....page 83

1. 35 minutes
2. 2:45 P.M.
3. two weeks (14 days)
4. April 3
5. 25 minutes

Time Conversions ....page 84

1.	30 years	6.	30 minutes
2.	365 days	7.	90 seconds
3.	180 seconds	8.	48 hours
4.	12 hours	9.	31 days
5.	14 days	10.	40 years

Perimeter.............page 85

1.	12 cm	6.	22 in.
2.	36 in.	7.	84 mm
3.	89 ft.	8.	72 yds.
4.	77 m	9.	33 m
5.	65 km		

Area ....page 86

1. 10 square units
2. 6 square units
3. 6 square units
4. 9 square units
5. 9 square units
6. 7 square units
7. 10 square units
8. 8 square units
9. 5 square units
10. 11 square units
11. 11 square units
12. 8 square units

Area and Perimeter.............page 87

Across
1. 211 (units)
3. 163 (units)
5. 22 (square units)
7. 111 (units)

Down
1. 20 (square units)
2. 141 (units)
4. 32 (square units)
6. 261 (units)

Area of Triangles, Rectangles, and Parallelograms ....page 88

1.	18	4.	50
2.	16	5.	9
3.	10	6.	9

Estimating Area ...page 89

1.	5	4.	5
2.	6	5.	14
3.	6	6.	9

What Is Volume? ....page 90

1. 5 cubes, 5 cubic units
2. 8 cubes, 8 cubic units
3. 9 cubes, 9 cubic units
4. 8 cubes, 8 cubic units
5. 10 cubes, 10 cubic units
6. 12 cubes, 12 cubic units

Find the Volume ..page 91

1. 12 cubic units
2. 24 cubic units
3. 30 cubic units
4. 18 cubic units
5. 8 cubic units
6. 24 cubic units
7. 25 cubic units
8. 16 cubic units

Using a Rule to Find Volume ....page 92

1. height = 4, length = 3, width = 1, 12 cubic units
2. height = 2, length = 4, width = 4, 32 cubic units
3. height = 3, length = 3, width = 2, 18 cubic units
4. height = 3, length = 1, width = 2, 6 cubic units
5. height = 2, length = 5, width = 1, 10 cubic units

Temperature ....page 93

1.	6° F	4.	28° F
2.	yes	5.	9° C
3.	63°F	6.	no

Temperature ....page 94

1. 59°F
2. 49°F
3. Tuesday and Thursday
4. Friday to Saturday
5. 10°F
6. 4°F
7. Wednesday
8. Monday to Tuesday

Measure Me ....page 95

1. 2.5 inches
2. 4 inches
3. 5.5 inches
4. 1 inch
5. 3 inches
6. 10 cm
7. 14 cm
8. 6 cm
9. 8 cm
10. 2 cm
pencil—18 centimeters
rubber eraser—2 inches
thumb tack—1 centimeter
paperclip—1.25 inches
tissue box—10 inches

Customary Units of Length ....page 96

1. 21 feet
2. 2 feet
3. 2 yards
4. 52,800 feet
5. 5 feet
6. 10 yards
7. 62 inches
8. 36 inches
9. 40 inches
10. 2,640 feet
11. 2 feet
12. 1 yard
13. 12 feet
14. 1 yard
15. 39 inches

Metric Units of Length ....page 97

1.	340 mm	4.	no
2.	yes	5.	5,000 m
3.	300 cm	6.	10 km

Selecting Appropriate Units (Metric).......page 98

1. d. grams
2. a. meters
3. h. milliliters
4. i. kiloliters
5. b. kilometers
6. c. centimeters
7. g. liters
8. f. kilograms
9. e. milligrams

	Mass	Capacity	Length
Metric	grams kilograms	milliliters kiloliters	meters centimeters
Customary	ounces pounds	fluid ounces quarts	inches yards

Customary Units of Capacity ....page 99

1. 9 quarts
2. 56 pints
3. 20 cups
4. 4.5 quarts
5. 12 teaspoons
6. 6 gallons
7. 80 fluid ounces
8. 32 fluid ounces
9. 32 tablespoons
10. 10 cups in 5 days, not enough to fill a gallon
11. 80 drops

Metric Units of Capacity ....page 100

1. 2 L
2. 60 L
3. 3,000 L
4. 100 daL
5. 40 daL
6. .5 L
7. 2 kL
8. 5,000 L
9. 7 kL
10. 420 L
11. 4.5 kL
12. 90 L
13. 5 kL
14. 5 bottles

Selecting Appropriate Units (Capacity) ....page 101

1. kL
2. kL
3. mL
4. L
5. mL
6. kL
7. mL
8. L
9. L
10. L
11. mL
12. L

Customary Units of Mass ....page 102

1. 32 oz.
2. 2.5 t.
3. 10 lbs.
4. 12,000 lbs.
5. 240 oz.
6. 320 oz.
7. 8 t.
8. 4 lbs.
9. 160 oz.
10. 32 oz.
11. 1.5 t.
12. no
13. yes

Metric Units of Mass ....page 103

1. 10,000 g
2. 10 dag
3. 2 kg
4. .5 kg
5. 7 t
6. 2,000 mg
7. 3,000 kg
8. 4.5 kg
9. 3 dag
10. 6 g
11. 40 kg
12. 5 hg
13. 10 stones
14. 35 cookies
15. 6 grams
16. 1,300 grams

Selecting Appropriate Units (Mass).......page 104

1. g
2. kg
3. kg
4. g
5. g
6. g
7. g
8. g
9. kg
10. kg
11. g
12. kg

Pictograph ....page 105

1. 57
2. theater
3. 12
4. no
5. zoo

Tally Chart ....page 106

1. 14
2. 29
3. Thursday
4. 100
5. Friday

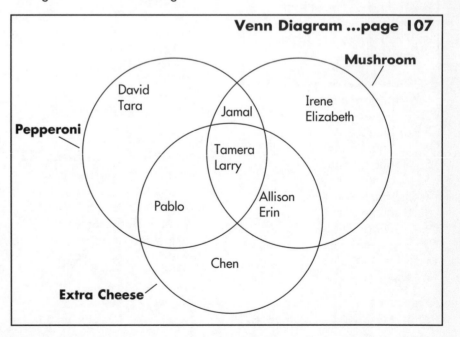

Venn Diagram ...page 107

Pepperoni — David, Tara

Mushroom — Irene, Elizabeth

Jamal

Tamera, Larry

Allison, Erin

Pablo

Chen

Extra Cheese

Glyph ....page 108

This person is a **boy** with **five** people in his family. To get to school, this person **walks**. This person was born in the month of **June**. At lunchtime, this person eats **in the cafeteria**.

Circle Graph ....page 109

1. 36
2. other board games
3. chess
4. same size
5. other board games
6. chess, other board games and checkers

Line Graph.................................page 110

1. The temperature rose and then fell. This could be explained by the rising and setting of the sun.
2. 5 degrees
3. 77°F (also could be 78°F), 1 P.M.
4. 65°F, 5 P.M.
5. between 1 P.M. and 5 P.M.

Median, Mode, and Range..................................page 112

1. median = 15, mode = 14, range = 8
2. median = 53, mode = 52, range = 10
3. median = 12, mode = 14, range = 9
4. median = 82, mode = 82, range = 11
5. median = 73, mode = 73, range = 8
6. median = 4, mode = 4, range = 7
7. median = 34, mode = 36, range = 5
8. median = 25, mode = 25, range = 27

Probable Outcomes ....page 113

1. 8
2. 1 out of 8
3. 4 out of 8
4. 1 out of 8
5. 4 out of 8
6. 8
7. a penny
8. 1 out of 8
9. 2 out of 8
10. 6 out of 8

Representing Data Different Ways ....page 111

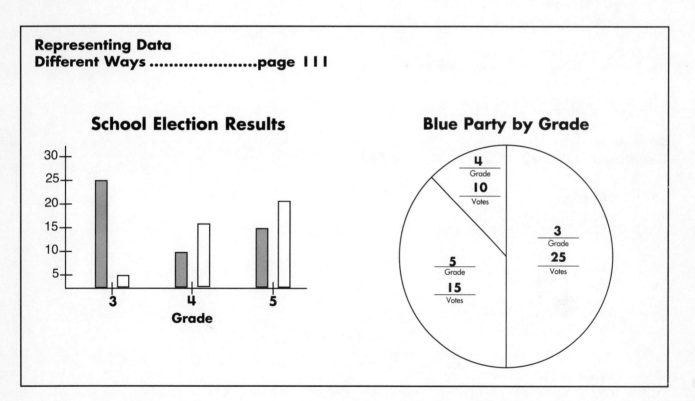

School Election Results

Blue Party by Grade

Probable
Outcomes ....page 114

1. 4 out of 8
2. 1 out of 8
3. 1 out of 8
4. 4 out of 8
5. 2 out of 8
6. 2 out of 8
7. 4 out of 8
8. 1 out of 8
9. 0 out of 8
10. 2 out of 8
11. 2 out of 6
12. 2 out of 6
13. 2 out of 6
14. 1 out of 6
15. 3 out of 6

Relative
Frequency.....................................page 115

1. 5 out of 24
2. 9 out of 24
3. 4 out of 24
4. 6 out of 24
5. 14 out of 24
6. 10 out of 24
7. 11 out of 24
8. 13 out of 24
9. 24 out of 24
10. 0 out of 24

Degree of
Likelihood.....................................page 116

1. yellow (3 out of 12), blue (2 out of 12), red (6 out of 12), green (1 out of 12)
2. red, green
3. add 1 green button or remove 1 blue button
4. She could make sure there are only 3 buttons of each color in the bag.
5. yellow (2 out of 11), blue (2 out of 11), red (6 out of 11), green (1 out of 11)

Degree of
Likelihood.....................................page 117

1. 6 out of 15
2. 4 out of 13
3. 5 out of 15
4. 4 out of 15
5. 1 out of 3